THE
COURAGE
TO
CONTINUE

NAVIGATING YOUR CORPORATE JOURNEY

CHERYL L. BEVELLE-ORANGE

BALBOA.PRESS

A DIVISION OF HAY HOUSE

Balboa Press books may be ordered through booksellers or by contacting:

Balboa Press
A Division of Hay House
1663 Liberty Drive
Bloomington, IN 47403
www.balboapress.com
844-682-1282

Print information available on the last page.

ISBN: 979-8-7652-2586-8 (sc)
ISBN: 979-8-7652-2587-5 (e)

Balboa Press rev. date: 10/27/2022

CONTENTS

DEDICATION

I DEDICATE THIS BOOK TO:

~The 21-year-old, young, Black woman who resembles the 21-year-old version of myself as she embarks upon a journey into the corporate world.

~To the young woman who is afraid of being far away from the comforts of home, fearful of failure, and terrified of being alone, navigating what society and circumstances has created for her.

~To the young woman who is sitting in her undecorated work cubicle wondering, *"What do I do now? Who can help me? Am I enough? Do I belong? Did I make the right decision?"*

~To all of the women above the older, wiser version of me will tell you to do everything you have dreamt of doing, talk to everyone in order to build a viable network, and take breaks when you need to replenish so you have the stamina to keep moving forward.

~And yes, YOU ARE ENOUGH! You made the right decision. Your parents and "village" are prouder than you can imagine. Stay focused and keep pressing on. If not for yourself, keep going for the next generation of young ladies who will stand on your shoulders and follow in your footsteps.

~Cheryl~

INTRODUCTION

My Personal Journey

It was the summer of 1990. I was young, bright-eyed, excited, and, like most 21-year-olds with a brand spanking new college degree under their belt, I was ready to explore and conquer the world!

As my 13-year-old brother, Michael, and I set off on a 35-hour, cross-country trek with our paper roadmap, in my Chevy Cavalier, driving from Bessemer, Alabama to Fairfield, California gave me mixed emotions churning in the pit of my stomach. I was excited and hopeful about my future, yet anxious and fearful of failure. I remember the faces of my parents and the sound of my mother, as she choked back tears, trying her best to utter the words "goodbye", not sure when she would see her baby girl again. The image of my parents and neighbors who had become my extended family and "village" is one forever ingrained in my psyche. Why? Because, for me, it marked the beginning of an era of "becoming."

Prior to that, the only other place I had ever ventured, outside of Alabama, was Detroit, Michigan, where we typically traveled for vacations, funerals, and family reunions. So imagine a young, naive, inexperienced, and impressionable Black girl relocating to the sunshine, blue skies, unpredictable, and fast-paced living the *golden state* of California offered. I was determined to be successful – equipped with a multitude of prayers, full tank of gas, $1,000 (from graduation gifts and savings), and the promise of a job paying $800 a week to carry me to my next step – whatever that was.

One of the seemingly trillion and one job applications I completed since earning my dual degrees, a B.A. in Marketing, and a B.S. in Computer Science from Jacksonville State University, landed me my first real corporate job. And while I had no real experience outside of working at Krystal's taking orders and being a hostess at a local restaurant, the job was ideal for my basic credentials and interests. I had hopes of exploring places other than Alabama and Detroit by traveling the world, someday.

Albeit far from what I now consider a corporate position, my first *real* job was as a Base Exchange Manager for the Army and Air Force Exchange Services (AAFES), also known as the BX. This position put me on the path to corporate success, prepared with some foundational lessons it taught me.

Fast forward, almost 30 years later, I am now Managing Director of Information Technology at a Fortune 500 transportation company and a leader in my industry. Through my career path spanning decades, I've gained experience in the areas of leadership, marketing, project/program management, strategy development and IT operations and governance.

My playbook of experience in breaking down barriers and climbing the countless steps on my personal ladder to success, inspired me to start documenting my journey nearly 25 years ago. As I prepared to publish my first book, the COVID-19 pandemic happened, which added an additional layer of knowledge to my databank. I gained a fresh, new perspective on how to thrive in the workplace. And while work as we know it has clearly changed, some of the fundamental aspects will always remain the same.

I am sharing lessons learned from situations I've experienced, encountered and studied so your task of traveling the corporate path won't be as daunting as it was for me. When I first started out, I had no idea how a corporate environment operated. The concepts I will outline in this book have been tested, tweaked and validated as I've mentored hundreds throughout my career and seen, firsthand, the results.

I can honestly say that writing this book has been a labor of love and cathartic for me as it allowed me to release my thoughts into a space where I initially had no one to talk to. It is lonely being the "ONLY." Many times I was either the only person of color, the only woman, or sometimes both. Through writing, I was able to debrief my experiences, reflect on certain scenarios and situations, and sometimes cry during moments of reflection.

My initial goal for documenting my journey was to ensure I equipped my two children with insight and ideas that would help them when they began their professional careers. My children are now all grown up, complete with college degrees and jobs. Unbeknownst to them, they were actual test studies on many of my concepts. My goal now is to support first-time corporate personnel by offering this guide to help them surf the potential rough waters of their careers more smoothly.

Complete with strategies and information, my hope is this book will provide valuable insight so you are not oblivious, naive, and unaware when navigating the structure of the corporate workplace. I encourage you, as a reader, to take this guide, study the contents and journal your thoughts, along the way. Documenting these will undoubtedly help you discover how to apply the tips, practices and tools outlined in this publication.

To all of the first-time, and even veteran, professionals who dare to read and apply this material, consider yourselves ahead of the game. Hang in there; do not give up and kudos to you for having the *Courage to Continue* your journey!

CHAPTER 1

CREATING YOUR CAREER ROADMAP

Belle Sumpter, Alabama or *Sumpter* as it was called by my aunts, was the "ruralist of rural." There were no street lights, traffic lights or satellite TV. Sumpter is where my journey began. I'd gather eggs in the morning from the chicken coop and ride the cows like horses in the afternoon. This was all I knew; this was normal to me. Boy was I in for an awakening.

At Oak Grove Elementary, I was different. Too light to be black and to black to be white. I was usually the ONLY person of color in my classroom. One of my elementary teachers, Ms. Betsy, had a porcelain arm. She knew how I felt because she was also the "only" one as well. Our bond was through both of us being the "only" and, ironically, she is the only teacher I remember from elementary school.

Education has always been very important to me. When I was in second or third grade, on one of my school off days, I was on my version of a "field trip" with my grandparents. We traveled to the bank, Burger King and back home. While in the bank, my grandfather was asked to sign his name on some documents. I saw him mark an "X" on one of the lines. My grandmother then signed her name on the line under his, which I now know was the "Witness" line.

Being the very curious and outspoken kid I was at the time, I asked my grandfather, "Grandaddy, why didn't you write your name?" Of course I was told, by my grandmother, to be quiet. Grandaddy never said a word. Instead, we went on to Burger King and then back to Sumpter.

That night, as I was doing my homework with my mother who was a second grade teacher, I shared with her what happened. She explained to me the history of the "X" and how Blacks who could not read or write used it as a representation of their name. Although I didn't realize it at the time, in retrospect, I can only imagine how humiliating and debilitating it must've been for my grandfather, a 60-year-old Black man, to not be able to read or write.

From that point on, education and learning, teaching and mentoring others have been at the core of who I am. Fast forward from the little girl in the bank to being the only African American cheerleader in high school, a girl who loved show choir, Country music, the Doobie Brothers, Earth Wind and Fire, Luther Vandross, Hall and Oates, Billy Graham, Clark Sisters, James Cleveland, and others artists who were unpopular with folks my age at the time. I played the clarinet and piano and watched The Lawrence Welch Show. I used to think, what a mess I am!

When I look at how and where I grew up and the lessons learned, I realize I was actually quite cultured. Those experiences taught me to embrace being different, to keep pushing forward no matter what, and to search for synergies and new ways of looking at situations. What I learned, at an early age, helped me to maneuver through life circumstances and understand the importance of looking at situations from different angles. All of these experiences were crucial in helping me build my toolbox for future "real life" scenarios, most of which I did not anticipate at the time.

One of the many tips I have acquired is to remain focused on a situation so you do not miss the lesson. This is essentially why I wrote this book, detailing scenarios I've either lived or witnessed, along with tips for being successful in not just the corporate world, but the REAL world. Whether you are just finishing college, starting a new job, changing careers, or just moving to a different department within your current organization, you will no doubt encounter corporate politics, office politics or business strategies as some refer to it.

Being a *first-generation* corporate professional simply means the individual is the first person in his or her family to work in a corporate environment, which defines many minorities, including me. A corporate employee is someone who holds a position in a company, organization, or corporation, which may be composed of several branches in different regions or global locations. Many of these jobs are in a hierarchical reporting structure and include managers at various levels. A few things to keep in mind about corporate positions:

- Usually competitive, but a favorable entry-level place to start, learn and develop your career.
- Great learning opportunities, but only if you take advantage of them.
- Typically offer good benefits because of significant savings due to bulk cost scales.
- Often strategically located in large cities in order to attract a more diverse group of employees.
- All positions are important to a corporation, no matter the level.
- The interview process for larger corporations may be lengthy, especially, for a higher-level position.

For me, coming from Sumpter, a city with a population of less than 75 people with the nearest store being ten miles away and where most people either knew or were related to one another, corporate America was very scary. I had no idea what to do or who to trust. I did not see this environment depicted on any of the three local stations I watched on our black and white TV. I was terrified, yet driven and, therefore, had the *courage to continue* on my journey.

My great grandparents were sharecroppers with land in Boligee, Alabama, set on the Tom Bigbee river. We often fished and had picnics there when I was a kid. One summer, my dad threw me in the river where I had to sink or swim. In hindsight, this was probably not a good idea, but my dad was right there to save me. Joining the ranks of a business professional has similarities to this same scenario. With no training or lessons, I felt as if I was thrown into the river all over again; only this time, it was up to me to fail or succeed. Nevertheless, it was an unnerving and somewhat frightening experience, but needless to say, I learned to tread water and managed to stay afloat as I am still here and thriving.

If you worked in any organization, large or small, you may have been faced with office or corporate politics. So, what are office or corporate politics? Good question. *Office politics* are behaviors employees use to increase the probability of obtaining positive outcomes for themselves within the organization. Office politics are not something you can opt out of when you do not like them. The truth is they are a spoken and unspoken part of every organization.

Corporate politics are a common part of the corporate culture; no matter your role, politics are all around. Again, you may say, "I'm not going to participate in this foolishness. I'm just going to do my job and it will work out." Well, that was my perception until I was confronted with situations where I had to look within to persevere.

Consider when you were a child, did your parents expose you to checkers, chess, dominoes, or any other strategy games? If so, perhaps you resisted playing because you weren't interested or thought of them as "nerd games." Well, in reality, these games were designed to challenge us to think and learn to be strategic in decision-making.

I actually enjoyed playing checkers but did not realize, at the time, how that experience marked the beginning of my learning key strategic techniques. In retrospect, had we, as kids, embraced these games, understood their core value and learned how to outplay our opponents, we would likely be more efficient at playing corporate politics. *You can't play the game if you don't understand the rules.*

CASE STUDY #1: UNDERSTANDING POLITICS IN THE WORKPLACE

Angela was nominated for a special assignment in her organization. At the time, she was a manager in the Marketing department at a Fortune 500 company. The director, who was her supervisor, had shared the assignment with her and informed her peer managers that she was moving to another assignment. Angela, in turn, informed her team that a transition was occurring and she would assume a new role. The senior vice-present was also in the loop and started the transition planning.

Within three days after Angela was notified, but before an official corporate announcement was released, everything changed. Another person with influence and who had a relationship with the final decision maker, was given the assignment. Angela was informed of this change.

The special assignment was given to someone else because they knew how to leverage relationships. It was not that the other person was more qualified, but because of their personal connections and organizational relationships, they had an advantage over Angela. The person wanted the position and knew how to use influence of an existing relationship to get the job. Angela was left out in the cold. Not having the network, influence, personal power, or knowledge to make sure the original decision could not be overturned left Angela devastated and embarrassed.

Angela's story is remarkably similar to mine, early on in my career. After my experience, I decided to examine my situation and change the narrative for my future growth. I created a strategy and began to plan and manage my own career.

Someone once told me that "good work gets you onto the playing field, but relationships get you the starting position." That may not be 100% true and there are differing opinions on this concept, but I believe that to rely only on your performance is not enough. You also need valuable relationships in order to excel.

Does Angela's story sound slightly familiar? If not, keep working. Without knowing how to maneuver within the corporate system, you may encounter an analogous situation. My experience fueled my passion for mentoring and coaching professionals on how to build political competency and find success in the workplace.

As I shared earlier, I am a first-generation corporate professional who has a personal arsenal of "war stories." I've mentored many others who consistently ask, "How can I be successful? What do I need to know to help me to survive in corporate America? How can I stay on top of my game?"

My response? There are no magic answers or silver bullets. Instead, I offer basic practices in hopes it will give them beneficial tools to use for their journey.

Within this publication, I will provide key concepts and strategies to provide you with a better perspective and insight, helping you to recognize how to effectively maneuver within your own environment. It starts with CREATING A ROADMAP as your path to success. It will be difficult without one.

EXERCISE #1: CREATE A ROADMAP

- **Know yourself and focus on YOU!** We all tend to see flaws in others before we see them in ourselves. Self-awareness is an important leadership skill. By focusing on yourself, you will discover personal strengths and opportunities (flaws). As you work to understand these traits, you can feel some sense of accomplishment in knowing you are developing the key skill of evaluation.

- After conducting an evaluation, you can discern which areas excite you and bring out your best work as well as those that do not. There are many self-help books available to assist you in defining your strengths. For instance after reading a particular book, I learned to compare how the world saw me versus what I thought I was portraying to the world.

- Seek out different perspectives to furnish a clearer picture of who you believe you are and how you are being viewed in your personal and professional life. The self-help book referenced earlier also discussed highlighting your strengths as opposed to only focusing on your flaws. Make sure you are competent enough in your opportunity areas (those that need improvement) and an expert in your strengths in order to effectively perform in your career. A good leader will find team members who can balance both strength and opportunity areas.

- You are in charge of your career. Create an action/career plan by answering, "Where do I want to be in 1 year, 3 years, 5 years, and 10 years?" This requires concentrated thought and planning.

- Develop goals and make sure they are measurable (how much and by when); make them specific (e.g., attend a toastmaster class by December); make them realistic (can I accomplish them?); and make them visible (place reminders on frequently seen items such as your computer or bathroom mirror).

Below is an example of a Roadmap/Career Plan you can review to aid in creating one for yourself. Within your plan, you should determine your goals, who you can/will ask for support, and how frequently you need to interact.

ROADMAP/CAREER PLAN

Instructions: Create a roadmap/career plan using the sample below as a guide. Use the blank form for your own roadmap.

Roadmap/Career Plan Example:

Goal	What role do I want to have within the organization?	What educational resources are required to reach this goal (i.e., degrees, special coursework, or certification). Do I need a development plan? (example below)	Are there people or connections within your organization available to help you achieve your goal(s)?	How often should I meet with the people listed in the previous column?
1-2 years	Release Train Engineer	Bachelor's degree RTE Certification	Charlie - Leader of the Agile Training Matt - My Manager	Once a week Once a month
3-5 years	Manager	Master's degree Management Basics Course Emotional Intelligence Class	Current Director - Donald Current VP - Scott	Once a month-happy hour Once a quarter
5-7 years	Director	May depend on company guidelines	Current VP - Scott Former VP - Tucker SVP IT - Tamara VP of Finance - Julie	Once a month Once a month - golf Twice a year Twice a quarter

Now, it's your turn!

Roadmap/Career Plan Worksheet

Name:
Date:

Goal	What role do I want to have within the organization?	What educational resources are required to reach this goal (i.e., degrees, special coursework, or certification). Do I need a development plan? (example below)	Are there people or connections within your organization available to help you achieve your goal(s)?	How often should I meet with the people listed in the previous column?
1-2 years				
3-5 years				
5-7 years				

The Career Plan you just completed is your "high-level" roadmap. Next, use the Individual Development Plan as a guide for implementing your roadmap.

Individual Development Plan Example

Development Goal: <u>To increase industry knowledge for improving core leadership skills.</u>

What strategies or steps can I take to get to the next level?	What is a realistic timeframe to accomplish the strategy or step?	How will I evaluate each strategy or step?	How will I know when the strategy or step is completed?
Understand Executive Presence Effective Leadership Through Radical Awareness Develop Business Acumen	*In the next 6 months I will read articles and books on executive presence and demonstrate behaviors.* *In the next 6 months I will become more self-aware by completing exercises to understand/document my strengths, weaknesses, and journaling daily.* *I will read books and news publications as well as listen to podcasts and webinars to enrich my understanding of the industry and obtain information to help with self-improvement.*	*Create a training schedule* *Ask direct supervisor, VP team members and peers to observe and share feedback*	*Feedback from supervisor and team members* *Demonstration of skills and competencies*

It's your turn. Create your own Individual Development Plan

Development Goal: _____

What strategies or steps can I take to get to the next level?	What is a realistic timeframe to accomplish the strategy or step?	How will I evaluate each strategy or step?	How will I know when the strategy or step is completed?

CHAPTER 2

THE POWER OF MENTORS, POWER PERSONNEL, ADVOCATES AND SPONSORS/CHAMPION

Congratulations! You just completed the first exercises towards, what I hope will be, your new path to corporate success. Now that you have a draft of your career roadmap and your development plan, let us take the next step in this journey. This chapter will outline the configuration of relationships you will need to help win the corporate game.

My First Mentor

Larry Ferguson was a bald, Caucasian gentleman, with blue eyes and a cheerful disposition. He recruited me from AAFES retail to the Electronic Data Interchange (EDI) department, which was a part of the Information Technology (IT) segment of AAFES. My early work in retail was great, as a first job, but getting up at dawn to open the store and closing late at night, interacting with customers and standing all day, took a toll. Some people are built for retail and some are not. I was NOT! However, sometimes, we do what is necessary in order to do what we want later. That is what retail was for me. It was the jumpstart to my career and a stepping stone in my corporate journey. I am grateful for my time in the retail space because it taught me so much.

When I started with AAFES, I underwent a stringent training program, where I learned every aspect of the store from operating the cash register, the opening and closing functions, learning soft lines (clothing), and hard lines (deodorants, toiletries, etc.). I was taught how to ship and receive from manufacturers, and from store to store, as well as how to work with planograms. Retail awarded me a perspective of appreciation for my first cubicle, computer, desk phone, an 8:00am – 5:00pm schedule, and all of the perks of a corporate office.

On my first day of work at AAFES corporate office, I believe Larry sensed my nervousness. I tried to behave as if I belonged, though I am sure my discomfort was written all over my face and in my body language. Larry introduced me to Brenda and others in the group, showed me to my cubicle, and left me to do all my first-day transfer paperwork. The next day, he brought me into his office and we began to talk about the corporate part of the company. He asked me about my family and shared about his. He talked me through my responsibilities and expectations, took me to lunch and spent time with me every day for six weeks. Looking back on it now, that was a lot of time to spend with one person, but Larry's approach involved thorough training on the front end, so that there was less to do, training-wise, on the back end.

Larry was my first mentor and a great one at that. Although he was old enough to be my father and, oftentimes, very curt in his approach, he became my mentor and my friend. My situation was unique because I did not seek out a mentor, it just happened. But for many, finding a mentor can be a chore.

What is a Mentor?

A mentor is a trusted counselor or guide that is experienced in his or her field of expertise. A mentor often shares details about their career path, and provides guidance, motivation, emotional support, and role modeling to the mentee. A mentor is someone you can talk to and receive feedback of how you are being perceived in the workplace. You should be able to share the good, the bad and the ugly, being totally transparent with your mentor without fear of judgement. This person can help you gain insight into what you need to do in order to do your job well. In addition, you should be able to talk openly to your mentor about how to position yourself for success within the organization.

Once you identify and secure a mentor, you should be able to utilize him/her to help you zoom in on both your strengths and blind spots, in order to help you to be successful. Through a simple Google search, you will find statistics and other information to support the notion that those who are mentored typically out-perform and out-earn those who are not. Also, those who are mentored get promoted more often and report lower burnout rates.

Having just one mentor can be limiting, so I recommend having a team of mentors to help put you in the driver's seat for your career. It is essential to have a personal mentoring team or collective. This collective should always have your best interest at heart and must be selected very carefully. A mentoring team can offer an assortment of ideas, perspectives, skills, and social capital. The more diversity within your team, the greater your reach and potential.

To visualize a team of mentors, think about a softball team. In the infield you have a first, second and third base position, as well as a pitcher and a shortstop. Each one has a specialized skill set and understand their role. In the same spirit, we should all have an infield of specialized mentors helping us to play the game efficiently.

To bring this concept home, your first baseman might be someone in Finance if you need help in that area. Your shortstop might be a person who understands the political landscape and can help you in that area. And finally, your pitcher might be an expert in execution should you need assistance there. Once you put your mentoring team together, focus on a few goals at a time so you aren't overwhelmed. Build or enhance your plan, build your mentoring team and monitor your progress.

Characteristics of a Mentor

When seeking a mentor, please keep the following characteristics in mind:

- Mentors should be candid and should give constructive feedback.
- Mentors should be honest.
- Mentors should know how to listen and be great sounding boards.
- Mentors should value diverse perspectives.
- Mentors should be knowledgeable in a variety of areas.
- Mentors should challenge you.
- Mentors should have empathy.

I was very fortunate and blessed to have Larry guide me through the first stretch of my career. My advice to you would be to quickly find a mentor. If you are a leader, I encourage you to help your team members, whether seasoned or new to the corporate environment, find a mentor. Better yet, be the mentor they need. Do not wait for the team member to ask. Step up and help coach them to success.

Who and What are Power Personnel?

Power personnel are individuals who have considerable influence within the workplace. Power personnel may or may not carry a title that carries influence, but they have the network and/or sponsorship to get information in the right hands to secure high profile projects, retain the best people for their project teams, and secure a budget to ensure success.

Most people do not get assigned to high-exposure projects by chance. And, many times, it is the critical influence of power personnel that places them in the position.

So how do you determine who power personnel are within your organization? This can be done through daily observation. For example, if you see someone who is always interacting with the senior leadership group and they are not a peer, they are probably power personnel. If you are not paying attention, you may miss the seemingly casual interactivity; however, if you are watching closely, it should be easy to see who these people are. You can also identify these power personnel by asking (and answering) these questions:

- Who is next to move up in the organization at your level and a level above you?
- Who is being discussed among upper management?
- Who is giving presentations at all the departmental meetings?
- Who gets the budgets to do high-profile projects?
- Who is playing golf with the group while you are at work?

Once you have answered these questions, seek out these people in an effort to build genuine relationships as you work to become a power professional within your organization.

Here are a few tips to put you in position as power personnel:

- Look at what and how power personnel conduct themselves and get things done.
- Take note of how they work, take notes, and use what you think will help.
- Invite one or more power personnel to lunch for a conversation of things you may have in common.
- Try to make a sincere connection. You want an organic relationship and not something forced.

EXERCISE #2 – Power Personnel Exercise

Who are the power personnel within your company? Take a few days to observe in meetings and listen to conversations to see who they are.

HINT: They may NOT be the people who are most vocal. Some of whom may try to portray themselves as important, may not be. Be aware.

INSTRUCTIONS: List the power personnel in your department (immediate group). Rank your identified power personnel by the likelihood of an opportunity to be approached. Remember, power personnel can help you identify successful behaviors you may want to mimic.

List the power professionals in your immediate work group

1. _____

2. _____

3. _____

4. _____

List the power professionals in your department (a level up)

1. _____

2. _____

3. _____

4. _____

What is an Advocate?

An advocate, in our context, *is anyone who speaks highly of another to others and seeks to create a positive opinion of that person.* Even better said, an advocate is someone who openly supports and recommends another. It is a good practice to find as many people as you can to advocate for you.

An example of advocacy is when you are asked to write a letter of recommendation. Doing so means you are advocating for that person. You want the decision maker to take the person you are advocating for seriously so you write a letter outlining all the positive qualities of that person.

I have had many advocates throughout my career; however, it takes time to build those relationships and basically prove yourself so they can positively advocate on your behalf. One person in particular that stands out as an advocate for me was Donald. I worked with Donald for years as a manager. And although his training process was hard, he pushed me to excellence on every project. After I left Donald's area, he was one I could always depend on to share the goodness of Cheryl.

Understand that while you may have your "positive advocates," there may also be "negative advocates." Negative advocates do the exact opposite of positive ones. And while you want to have as few negative advocates as possible, they can play a critical role in your professional development. They can challenge you to be better. Creating a negative advocate is easier than creating a positive one. Just have a bad day; show lack of emotional intelligence with a response during a meeting; be harsh in an email unnecessarily; or miss a deadline to deliver by not being more flexible and innovative. All of these scenarios may create negative advocates.

Take some time and think about this concept. Exercise #4 at the end of this chapter will help you document positive and negative advocates. Once you identify the negative ones, think through how to overcome them.

What is a Sponsor or a Champion?

A sponsor or champion in the corporate business world is someone who stages, introduces and publicly supports another person. They purposefully let others know about qualifications and traits of a person (e.g., "Have you thought about Cheryl for this project? Put Cheryl in and she can get it done.") They can introduce you to others in order to help create beneficial opportunities. Your sponsor should:

- Be at a senior level (VP or C-level) within your organization
- Champion you by being able to clearly articulate your strengths
- Advocate for you when others are unjustly blocking your progress
- Function as a role model who has "walked the walk"
- Value diversity and inclusion

Sponsors or Champions in Action

Once I interviewed for a promotion and felt confident during the process. One of my colleagues, Thaun, helped me for weeks to prepare for the interview. Thaun was in HR and very experienced with the process. During my lunch hour, we would prep with questions and responses. For some of the more common questions, he asked that I send my answers to him for review. He advised me to practice in the mirror so I could see my facial expressions when I responded and to record myself to hear how I sounded. After these practice sessions, I concluded there is really an art to interviewing. Do not underestimate how much your peers can help you so do not be afraid to ask for assistance when needed.

After I had gotten the job, I heard that my sponsor, Tom, made a call on my behalf to the hiring leader. He also made a point to talk with the leader at a subsequent meeting. The words they used were, "Tom did a full court press on your behalf." This is what sponsors do. They help open doors for their proteges and put in 110% effort to "sell" your qualities. However, they will not do this unless they honestly believe in you and your abilities.

CASE STUDY #2: FINDING A SPONSOR WITHIN A COMPANY

During my research, I encountered a young lady who was promoted to an executive role at a Fortune 100 company before she was thirty. She shared with me that before her promotion she had a list of people (power personnel and sponsor candidates) with whom she wanted to network. She strategically planned and prepped by examining how her projects could potentially impact those power personnel and sponsor candidates in various areas. She had intentional conversations to make connections, which would, hopefully, generate a positive opinion of her. When it was time to fill the executive position, she called on those people she had built relationships.

It looks simple on paper but it takes genuine work and effort to cultivate these relationships. Look at the roadmap you created earlier as a plan for your career. This plan should also include social gatherings such as golf tournaments, happy hours, and lunches. Being present and seen at these events can keep you top of mind when promotions and special assignments become available. Now with a hybrid environment, we have to be relevant on zoom meetings and set up zoom happy hours to connect. Connection is the key. When your sponsor mentions you in the meeting, others should shake their heads in agreement. You must have strong relationships so those in decision making positions know you, your work and can say, "Yes, she/he deserves the chance and can do the job." If you do not put in deposits, as Covey states in his *7 Habits of Highly Effective People*, into work relationships you will not be able to take anything out.

NOTE: Genuine connections must be made; people can tell when you are not authentic.

Networking Matters

Network with everyone; you never know who can help you or who you can help along your career path. Create alliances with all levels of personnel including administrative support, janitors, leadership, cafeteria personnel, etc.

Networking is something I have learned to appreciate. A few years after I started my first corporate position, I moved from Larry and that company to a new organization. I was still in a corporate environment but I had no mentor and networking was part of this new culture.

Being an introvert, I was content sitting in my cubicle working on my computer. In my mind, doing a great job would get me noticed and that was all the networking I needed. Wrong! My introverted self was very misguided. As I sat in my cubicle, I saw others move from position to position and get promotions. I often wondered why because I had received accolades for doing excellent work.

It turns out, I had not expressed my desire to grow and develop within the company. I had not shared my career plan with my boss. I also did not have a mentor like Larry. In the next chapter, we will talk about how I strategically found a mentor, but I wanted to share this story because, as an introvert, it was HARD to break out of my norm and proactively reach out.

EXERCISE #3 – MENTOR JOURNALING EXERCISE

INSTRUCTIONS: Take a moment to journal, answering these basic questions:

Who are your mentors? If you do not have a mentor(s), who should you pursue as a mentor?

Who is your sponsor or advocate? If you do not have a sponsor or advocate, who should you pursue?

Many people use the words *mentors* and *sponsors* interchangeably. Mentors and sponsors both provide guidance and advice to help develop future leaders. They also help to create a diverse workplace and are key to successful career advancement, but mentors and sponsors are quite different. Use the space below to write down your mentors, sponsors and advocates and your major thoughts:

_____

_____

_____

_____

_____

_____

_____

_____

_____

In this chapter, we also talk about power personnel and advocates and how they are needed as well. But if I had to rank importance, I would list mentors and sponsors/ champions at the top. I would like for you to have clear view of the differences between mentors and sponsors so I created the "At A Glance" chart below:

Mentors & Sponsors At A Glance

Mentors give advice and have mentees	Sponsors/Champions are the lead advocate and have protégés
Mentors have experience in an area in which you want to develop your skills	Sponsors/Champions are senior level and invested in a person's career
Mentors support through formal or information discussions about skill building and career advancement	Sponsors/Champions are more formal and use their influence and networks to connect you to high-profile assignments, people, and promotions
Mentors help craft career plans/ vision and development plans	Sponsors/Champions help drive career plans/vision
Mentors give suggestions on how to expand their mentee's network	Sponsors/Champions give access to their active network connections and make new connections on their behalf
Mentors give insight on how to increase visibility	Sponsors/Champions promotes visibility, often using their own "political capital"
Mentors share "unwritten rules" for advancement	Sponsors/Champions can share "unwritten rules" but they actively model behavior and involve their protégé in experiences (projects/initiatives) that could enable career advancement
Mentoring can be a two-way street	Sponsoring/Champions is not a two-way street

To give you a personal example, I had a desire at one time to move from the IT organization back to the marketing organization. My mentor introduced me to relevant marketing articles, podcasts, and other training to help refresh my knowledge of the marketing discipline. My sponsor, on the other hand, helped me by virtually introducing me to the chief marketing officer (CMO) so she could become familiar with me and the best places to use my talents on the marketing leadership team.

We will talk more about mentors, advocates, and sponsors/champions in a future chapter, but as a recap:

- Mentors are those that help you with your day-to-day journey, development plans, and give you feedback. A mentor helps you to think through what you need to navigate your career more effectively.
- Positive advocates publicly support you by saying flattering things to others so they have a positive impression of you while negative advocates challenge you to stay at the top of your game.
- Sponsors or Champions are senior level people who are aware of your abilities and strengths and should proactively support you in senior management decision-making. They should also serve to help pave the way and open doors that may otherwise be unknown or closed. A sponsor/champion is someone who will ultimately help to create opportunities for you.

I sometimes use a choir analogy when I am speaking about the importance of soliciting mentors and other "support" in one's career journey. This might not resonate with everyone, but I hope you get the picture. Mentors are those who will help get you to the venue so the choir or advocates can sing your praises. Once you are in a place where the position is attainable, the choir or advocates, will be the ones who sing your positive praises to anyone who will listen. You will need the right people to sing your praises, at the right times. Power personnel can also can also play the role of advocates. Sponsors/champions are your lead singers because they will be the ones who make the calls that ultimately lead to open doors.

Exercise #4: POSITIVE AND NEGATIVE ADVOCATES

Really think through the information within this chapter. It will probably be easy to identify positive advocates; however, there are negative advocates as well, some you want to address and others you may not. The key is, knowing which category they fall into. This exercise will give you the opportunity to think about how you might strategically address them, should they become a concern.

Examples:
Positive Advocates

Current Positive Advocates	Positive Advocates to Pursue & Why
Brian - CEO	Anthony, SVP -IT – Brilliant mind and can learn how to think larger scale
Scott, SVP - Marketing	Brie, EVP -Marketing – Very well connected

Negative Advocates

Negative Advocates	Negative Advocates I want to Address
Jerod, VP, Ops	Yes – work with him more closely on the security project, set up one-on-one meetings to discuss issues and concerns prior to the official update meeting. This will help him to build confidence in what is being done and can help get him out of the negative advocate column.
Jonny, Mgr - IT	No- will not address

INSTRUCTIONS: Use the above example, find a quiet space, and take time to complete the chart below.

Positive Advocates

Current Positive Advocates	Positive Advocates to Pursue & Why

Negative Advocates

Negative Advocates	Negative Advocates I want to Address

CHAPTER 3

STRATEGICALLY SEEKING A MENTOR, ADVOCATE AND SPONSOR/CHAMPION

Now that you have clearly identified whether a mentor, advocate, sponsor/champion, or all of the above, will benefit you, it is now time to strategize on how to approach the individual(s). Determining the best approach will vary by person.

Mentorship is key to learning, growing, and progressing. I was extremely blessed that my first mentor, Larry, took the time to advise and guide me, especially at a time when I did not even know what a mentor was. In retrospect, I now realize I have had many mentors, some sought after and some not, throughout my life.

I am a "PK" or preacher's kid, and most of my early life was spent in church. I learned to play piano, mostly by ear. And what I did not learn on my own, Veronica Caldwell, the church pianist, taught me. We spent time together before and after church where I learned the "ins and outs" of playing gospel music.

Veronica was talented, kind and patient, showing me proper hand placement to play cords and beats on Sunday mornings. This skill helped pay my way through college as I served as minister of music at several local churches. Veronica also taught me there was room for everyone as she allowed me to play alongside her. She did not feel threatened I would take her job or outshine her; she poured into me until I was able to soar on my own. Veronica was one of my first mentors.

My first example of a Black woman in a corporate environment was Carol Davis. She was more of a role model to me, but she also "unintentionally" mentored me by the way she carried herself and personified the ultimate professional Black woman. She worked for a technology company in their Electronic Data Interchange (EDI) department.

Carol was the first African American corporate executive I had ever seen. She was always dressed to the nines; every hair in place with a stylish tapered cut; nails polished to match her lipstick; and carrying a designer handbag with coordinating classic pumps. Carol reminded me of Lena Horne because of her style and grace. I naturally gravitated toward her, wanting to find out exactly what she did so I could emulate her. I was truly fortunate that while I was still in high school, I was able to spend summers with her in Detroit and receive the informal mentoring she provided.

When I entered college in 1986, I majored in Computer Science, and landed my first IT job in EDI in 1993. Again, Larry was my first corporate mentor and I did not have to find him. But at other times throughout my career, I had to seek out mentors.

Once, I was leading a cross-functional, high profile project that had a heavy financial component. I understood the financial element at an elevated level but lacked an intimate relationship with numbers, which was critical to my role. As such, I had to find someone who could explain in detail what I needed, so I created a list of the power personnel within the Finance department.

After reviewing my list, I selected a gentleman named Jack because I could trust him to take the necessary time to teach me what I needed to know. I asked Jack to mentor me. We worked together for four weeks where he taught me a skill set that has benefitted me for years.

Finding a Mentor

There are several categories of mentors you should consider during your search, which I have listed below to assist you with securing a mentor. Once you have completed your roadmap and individual development plan as outlined in Chapter 1, you should be able to identify which mentor is best for your needs.

First, look to see if your company has a formal mentoring program. If so, sign up. You will be paired with someone and can get the ball rolling. If there is no formal mentoring program at your company, start small. Ask your direct manager or a team member for assistance on a project or assignment. This will give you an opportunity to get to know the person better, which may evolve into a mentor relationship. The person should be someone you have studied and their work or career is something you genuinely want to emulate. Once you have completed working together, ask if you could share your development and career plans and ask if they are willing to mentor you. Listed below are the most commonly used mentors for business development.

- *Peer Mentors* may be at the same level as you are but have a little more experience within the company or discipline. Peer mentoring can be powerful and very actionable.

  o Peer mentors can be internal to your department or work at the same company. They can also be external to the company but work in the same discipline.

  o How do you find a peer mentor? Sometimes a peer will be assigned to you when you join a company to help you onboard and get acclimated. If they are assigned, most of the time the person has volunteered and willing to help in any way. If the two of you are a good fit, continue that relationship. If a peer mentor is not assigned to you, think about your current workgroup. Who do you go to for help? Who answers your questions and brainstorms with you? That person has organically become your peer mentor. You can make it official or not, but the important thing is that the relationship has been formed and you are getting the guidance you need.

- *Traditional mentors* are usually those who are more senior. They are typically older and have a wealth of experience within the discipline or company. The traditional mentor is usually in management or leadership. Traditional mentors can be internal or external, just as the peer mentor.

  o How do you find a traditional mentor? If you have a good working relationship with your manager, he/she can initially become your traditional mentor; however, I would suggest getting an additional mentor as well. Is there someone in leadership that you admire? If so, ask them to be your mentor. The traditional mentor is one with whom you should share your development plan and career goals in order to receive career guidance.

- *Reverse mentors* are younger mentors. They can help with understanding new trends. Although this type of mentor may be younger, they typically have more experience than you in a certain discipline (e.g., social media). Again, reverse mentors can be internal or external. I often use my young adult children and their friends as my reverse mentors for guidance with some of the cultural trends and recent technology in the workplace.

  o How do you find a reverse mentor? Are there young millennials and GenZ'ers at the office you find to be future shining stars? If so, strike up a conversation about a topic of interest. Invite them to coffee to get to know them. They are usually eager to share whatever they know and contribute to the department and company. Other places to find reverse mentors are community and civic events.

With the knowledge Larry provided me as my mentor, my career took off. I was quickly promoted from individual contributor to manager. As my career progressed, I found I needed more of a mentoring team, in order for me to continue to grow. So I developed an action plan to help with this goal.

1. I decided which departments or areas I might want to be promoted to or rotate through.
2. I researched who the senior leaders were in those areas.
3. I determined what skills and/or relationships I needed from each.
4. I requested 15-minute meetings with each of them. See the conversation guide below:

5 minutes	Introduce myself briefly and share why I selected them as a mentor
5 minutes	Allow mentor to share his/her background
5 minutes	Discuss my individual development plan and goals of the relationship. Establish an on ongoing 30-minute meeting cadence.

Using the above approach, I was able to determine who I had an immediate connection with and who I might need to build one. I was also able to construct my team of mentors and establish how frequently I would meet with them. I asked each of them to play a specific role on my mentor team, and they agreed. Due to the nature of my role at the time, my mentor team was made up of a senior leader who understood the political landscape, someone who understood the compliance domain, and another senior leader who was in the information technology (IT) area.

Exercise #5: FINDING A MENTOR

Based on the information above and looking at your individual development plan from Chapter 1, think about what type of mentor you need to get to the next level of your career.

Finding a mentor exercise example

	Needed	Internal Or External	Names or comment
Peer Mentors	(YES) or No	(Internal) or External	Marc B.
Traditional Mentors	(YES) or No	(Internal) or External	Rita C.
Reverse Mentors	YES or (No)	Internal or External	I am the reverse mentor

INSTRUCTIONS: Use the example above along with your individual development plan and complete the chart below.

Finding a mentor exercise worksheet

	Needed	Internal Or External	Names or comment
Peer Mentors	YES or No	Internal or External	
Traditional Mentors	YES or No	Internal or External	
Reverse Mentors	YES or No	Internal or External	

If you are a mentor reading this book, it is critical to seek resources and training to be successful in your mentoring role. Thoroughly learning your role as a mentor will help you establish expectations for both you and your mentee. Below are a few characteristics, traits, and responsibilities of both a mentor and a mentee:

Mentors
• **Provides insight and exposure to the roles and responsibilities of a leader**
• **Share real life situations, past experiences, and best practices**
• **Be a confidant for the mentee**
• **Prioritize your mentee and mentoring sessions**
• **Share your communication style to help with information exchange**
• **Be honest and open to learning**
Mentees
• **Attend and be prepared for the meetings. Have an agenda so the meeting will be productive**
• **Share your communication style to help with information exchange**
• **Be honest, open to learning and hearing uncomfortable feedback**
• **Prioritize mentors time. Mentors sometimes have busy schedules. Be respectful.**

CASE STUDY #3: UNDERSTANDING THE MENTOR/MENTEE RELATIONSHIP

When the mentor/mentee relationship is a good match there is usually mutual benefit for both parties. I have found, as a mentor, I often receive nuggets of what not to do from my mentee and those nuggets make me a better leader. While I was completing this book, one of my mentees was a college sophomore. We worked on her interviewing skills and I coached her to land her first internship with a Fortune 500 company. As she finished the program, she wrote me the following note, *"Thank you for the great opportunity you brought my way, which will help me to be successful in life. I really appreciate you. You are the best mentor I've ever had. Enjoy your day!"* This was a sign of a good mentor/mentee match. Not all mentors and mentees are well matched. If you are creating an official mentoring program, have a confidential process to request a new mentor in case you did not match well. When you try to force a mentor/mentee relationship, it can do more damage than good.

Male vs. Female Mentors

In my over 25+ year corporate career, I have found it beneficial to have both female and male mentors. Here are some of the reasons why:

- Because it just makes good common sense!
- For a female, having a male mentor who has been identified as "power personnel" is a smart move. They are generally engaged and usually understand how to successfully maneuver within the confines of a business. Most of them have been playing "politics" most of their lives by using skills learned by participating in competitive sports.
- For a male, having a female mentor is a promising idea because she can offer a different perspective. She can convey different situations and obstacles she encountered in her career. Being an African American woman, I can also share stories of sexism and racism that others may not be able to share. I do not tell these stories often but I do impart what I have learned and techniques used to navigate through those scenarios.

CASE STUDY #4: MENTORING SUMMARY SHARED DURING A HIGHER EDUCATION LEADERSHIP ROUNDTABLE

In 2022, UC Berkeley had an Edge in Tech leadership roundtable where I was a speaker. I summed up a discussion on mentoring with the following information.

- Mentors are a guiding force for mentees seeking to understand new environments
- Mentorship programs need to focus on recruiting mentees
- Mentors help mentees in determining their vision for work
- Mentorship programs bring individuals together to think about where the gaps in equity within the organization exist
- Mentors help explain unwritten rules and corporate norms
- Mentors provide nudges and confidence boosts to help individuals in corporate settings
- Mentorship programs need metrics to measure success

Identifying Advocates

As a reminder, in Chapter 2, an advocate was defined as *"anyone that speaks highly of another to others and seeks to make others have a positive opinion of that person."* There are three types of corporate advocates:

1. **Self-Advocate**
2. **Peer Advocate**
3. **Senior Advocate**

What is Self-Advocacy?

Later in the book we will talk about self-promotion, which is a form of self-advocacy, which is about increasing awareness of work you and your team are doing. When you are your own self-advocate, you must have a strategy and/or frame for the narrative to allow others to see your value and "shine."

What is a Peer Advocate?

Peer advocacy is immensely powerful. If you recall the choir analogy, the backup singers or choir are your advocates. Peer advocates are your equals or peers, and ones who will campaign for and recommend you to be a part of their project teams. These team members are ones you have helped to become successful in the past by doing your job or going above and beyond to get things done with excellence. Good relationships with your peers is particularly important because some of them will excel up the corporate ladder with you and will continue to be your peers. Fostering those relationships is critical because you never know who you will need to work with in the future.

What is a Senior Advocate?

Senior advocates are personnel in senior ranks. In many instances, you may have helped deliver an initiative thus allowing them to see your work. They are the leaders in the senior level meetings backing up your sponsors or champions. You need these individuals as well.

Advocates and Sponsor/Champions in Action

A meeting occurs to determine the next lead of a major initiative. You are not in the meeting but your sponsor or champion is in attendance. You want them to mention your name as a potential leader; your senior advocates chime in, adding their support. When the other senior leaders return to their respective departments and inquire about you, you want your other advocates to have positive things to say. When the decision is finally made, you want to be the leader that has all positive feedback. Even if you are not the one selected to lead this initiative, you are set up for the next one.

How to be an Advocate

Most of what I have shared involves others advocating for you; however, there are opportunities when you can serve as an advocate for someone. Being an advocate is a powerful position. When you are an advocate, it means you are in a position to give council and your opinion matters.

Women in the corporate world, should support, recommend, aid, and publicly give credit to other women as well as be advocates for one another. "Allyship" can be a critical component in success for women as they progress in their careers. We must work together to advance the collective. The same concept of allyship applies to men of other men.

EXERCISE #6 – ADVOCATE JOURNALING EXERCISE

INSTRUCTIONS: Take a moment to journal. Answer these basic questions: Who are your advocates? How can you be an advocate for others?

_____

_____

_____

_____

_____

_____

_____

_____

_____

_____

_____

_____

_____

Finding a Champion or Sponsor

In business today, on most important projects, you will have an executive champion or sponsor. The champion breaks down barriers and paves the way because he/she believes in the project and its value.

Just as major projects need an executive champion or sponsor, you need a personal champion or sponsor who is an executive or someone at a senior level. Your sponsor is the person who speaks up for you in the decision-making environment. This is someone you trust and who offers your name as a leader and a person ready for that next big project, the next rotation or promotion.

A sponsor has several responsibilities but, in my opinion, there are four primary responsibilities you should understand, and align with your sponsor early in the process. Responsibilities of a Sponsor or Champion:

- To believe in and go out on a limb for their protégé
- To use their organizational capital, both behind closed doors and publicly, if needed, to push for their protégé's promotion or to lead major projects
- To provide organizational navigation support
- To provide their protégé with "air cover" for risk-taking. Meaning to shield them when they are exploring innovative ideas. [2]

So, how do you find a Sponsor or Champion?

- Sometimes sponsorship comes without effort. A senior leader notices your potential via the work you are doing or have done; they feel connected to you and the relationship begins. They may offer to have regular discussions.
- Sometimes it is incumbent upon you to search for and secure sponsorship for whatever reason.

  o The first thing I would suggest is to reflect on the initiatives you are currently leading. Do you have any interaction with the executive champion of the initiative? If so, use that connection to update the executive sponsor/champion. Share some of the ideas you have concerning the project and help her/him get to know you and your work. From there, if you have done or are doing an outstanding job with the project, you could ask them to sponsor you.

o Secondly, reflect on previous initiatives where you have had interaction with key executives. Reach out to inquire about possible stretch assignments, lateral and/or promotional opportunities.

o The third thing I would suggest is to list those executives you think might be great sponsors. Ask for a few minutes to talk with them about their background and career journey. From there, determine if you feel a connection and whether you want to nurture it further to a point where you ask them to sponsor you if it feels like a good fit.

CASE STUDY #5: UNDERSTAND WHY NAVIGATIONAL SUPPORT (OR ALLYSHIP) FROM SPONSORS FOR WOMEN IS NECESSARY

According to research from the Center for Talent Innovation (CTI), a non-profit think tank, the vast majority of women (85%) and multicultural professionals (81%) need navigational support to advance in their careers but receive it less often than Caucasian men. However, a 2010 *Catalyst* blog study revealed that more women than men have been assigned mentors yet 15% more men won promotions. Why? The findings indicated that having more mentorship did not lead to advancement but having a senior leader in a position to provide sponsorship did. As stated before both sponsors and mentors are important.

Exercise #7: IDENTIFYING POTENTIAL SPONSORS OR CHAMPIONS

Think about current or previous initiatives where you had a leading role.

Who are the executives that could be potential sponsors?
Who are those you have connected with before?
Who are those that you would like to connect with?

Once you work through the exercise below, put together a plan to keep the connections going and then, when you are comfortable, ask for sponsorship.

Sponsorship Grid Example

Initiatives	Potential Sponsors	Already Connected?	Need Connection?
Example: New Product Development (Robot)	CEO - Philips	Yes	No
Example: Enterprise Business Agility	SVP Hood	No	Yes

INSTRUCTIONS: Complete the grid below to identify potential sponsors or champions. Determine if you are already connected to them or if you need to make the connection. This is a valuable tool to work with your traditional mentor(s) to receive feedback and additional guidance. Once you have completed the grid, the next step is to determine how you will connect with those where you need a connection. Remember, if there is no action, there are no results.

Sponsorship Grid Worksheet

Initiatives	Potential Sponsors	Already Connected?	Need Connection?

Now that you identified your potential mentors and sponsors or champions, it is time to take action in solidifying their participation in your career journey. Use the steps identified within this chapter to ask for help.

As we close out this chapter, I'll leave you with a few final thoughts:

Please do not ask someone to be your sponsor if you are not performing at the level expected by your leadership. You should be at the top of your game and ready to take your career to the next level. If your game is weak, concentrate on doing a respectable job where you are, promote your work to your leadership team and start to position yourself by asking your boss, "What else do I need to do to have your support?" This will take time and effort. Do the work!

When thinking about the mentor/advocate/sponsor concepts, remember the choir example. Your sponsor is the soloist or lead singer, singing your praises all around in a loud voice. Your advocates and mentors are the backup singers sharing in harmony with others. Together, they form the group who brings awareness of your qualities, skills, and the wonderful things you have done in the workplace, showcasing how you can excel in the future.

CHAPTER 4

LEADERSHIP SUPPORT AND HONING YOUR SKILLS

Shortly after becoming a manager in 1999, I was selected to work on a startup initiative. My vice president (VP) commented he chose to work directly with me because he had confidence in me and had faith that I could get the initiative to market. My VP was the champion of the project but also served as my champion until he retired. However before he selected me, he talked with my immediate manager to get feedback which helped solidify my selection.

Securing mentors, sponsors, or champions, and identifying advocates is important for your career sustainability and growth. When going through the alignment and commitment process with your mentors or champions, they may reach out to your immediate supervisor to ask about you, just as my VP did.

The support of your immediate manager is important to your success in securing mentors and sponsors. If your immediate manager is not willing to support you, work is needed to either change that relationship or to move from under that chain of command. Your manager, unless you are at a senior level, will not typically serve as your mentor or sponsor. But then again he or she could be, like in the case of Larry. If you find that your immediate leader does not support your desire to progress, the following may be a few reasons why:

Your immediate leader or manager does not have confidence in your ability
Your immediate leader or manager may be insecure with their position and focused on his or her own career or agenda. They do not understand that working with his/her team can help advance their career as well
Your immediate leader or manager is gaining his/her "true" position

If you determine the situation with your current manager needs to change, using these tactics below may help improve your relationship.

- Nurture your relationship. Begin conversations outside of the office. Invite him/her to lunch; talk about things outside of work. You may find something you have in common as well as what is important to him/her.
- Look at things from his/her point of view. Take into account their position or opinion about things.
- Determine his/her communication style. Perhaps you are opposite or just alike. Either situation can cause undue friction so trying to work it out is the best course of action. There are many available tools to help in this area. Learning to communicate appropriately will benefit this relationship greatly.
- Identify what needs to occur so you both are aligned and "singing from the same page." When you are assigned a task, make sure you do the following:

  o Own it - Own the task, the initiative, and the results (good or bad)
  o Lead the effort of breaking down barriers to get to the desired outcome
  o Communicate your progress regularly
  o Assess your contribution to the strained relationship. Do not make the same mistakes twice. If everyone has the same issue with you, it would be advantageous to self-evaluate for corrective measures.

If you are a leader, you need emotional intelligence in order to recognize when there is a strain on a relationship with someone on your team. Sometimes we, as leaders, have to step up and realize our contribution to the situation. I ask you the question, "Are you being the leader you desire to be?"

CASE STUDY #6: HOW TO VISUALIZE LEADERSHIP ACCOUNTABILITY IN ACTION

During one instance of my career, I asked a direct report multiple times for a deliverable. The back and forth of making the same request repeatedly was exhausting. After a few missed dates, I asked myself, "How am I contributing to our lack of success?"

- As I reviewed the timeline of events, I examined the tasks I assigned along with the information provided for analyzing to see if I could have been clearer with my expectations or given more time to complete the task.
- I put the information in a consumable format and invited the team member to lunch. After our uncomfortable start, I brought up my observation, shared my analysis, and talked through what I thought was happening. I followed this by asking for her thoughts. She began crying and sharing how she felt unappreciated and overworked. Because of the situation, she was actually looking for another job.
- We collaboratively discussed how I could communicate more effectively and how she could ask clarifying questions to ensure she understood the ask.
- We planned to meet more frequently (30-minute check-in meetings weekly) to talk and align.

This sounds practical but the team member was thankful for the accountability and time I took to analyze how we could work better together. Because of these steps, she and I worked together successfully for another five years.

If you have an acceptable relationship with your immediate supervisor, think through how to make it better. Determine how you can move the needle forward to give him/her more confidence in you and speak to your strengths and weaknesses fairly when you are not in the room. Here are a few other tips/pointers:

- Show up to work on time. Whether you are showing up in person or on zoom; be on time and pay attention.

- Wear appropriate attire when on zoom (DO NOT WEAR PAJAMAS. I have seen it!)
- You may opt to assume some projects where she/he need assistance in completing. If you do, make sure you DELIVER.
- Volunteer for other assignments. Be sure you strategically select extracurricular activities you are passionate about as well as those that have networking opportunities.
- Take on the most challenging assignments to show you are a team player and that you can get things done. Some assignments may seem overwhelming at first glance; however, if you break it down into parts, you can make it manageable.
- Forward notes from others acknowledging your exceptional work to your supervisor. If someone verbally shares with you a compliment, do not be ashamed to ask them to send it to you in email.
- Seek out a high-profile project or a volunteer assignment. This will show the management team you can do the work.
- Do not only give minimum effort unless you only want to receive minimum recognition. Some projects take a long time to implement so make sure as you are documenting milestones within your project timelines, planning to have at least two big occurrences.
- Share your successes with your mentor and your sponsor.

You are responsible for your actions and cannot change anyone but yourself. If you know you are being efficient in your work and your immediate manager does not support you, try your skills in another group.

Review these examples of how you may be able to position yourself to move to another group if you think you are doing a great job, but not getting the support or career traction you believe you deserve:

- o Suggested dialogue: "I've been in this area for 3 years and I think it's time for a job rotation so I can continue to sharper by skill set."
- o If there are other jobs within the organization, apply for them.
- o Ask your sponsor for guidance on what group you should target to gain more experience.

o   If you really have someone in power you can trust, ask for a rotation.

o   If a rotation is not available, you may need to interview for an internal or external position. Take times to read the next section about interviewing for tips.

Behavioral Interviewing Tips To Help Prepare You For Your Next Interview

I have delivered many interviewing skills workshops and helped college students and professionals prepare to get the job they desire. Below are a few general behavioral interviewing tips to consider as you prepare for your next interview.

Before the interview: Do your research

- Talk to the leadership team if the job is internal or the recruiter, if external. Also, if external, research the company. Look at their company website and search for the leadership on LinkedIn or other social media to understand challenges, points of view and ideals the company represents. Review the job posting and qualifications needed. The information within the posting are clues to what is important in the job and can help you understand what questions may be asked during the interview. For example, if the posting asks for someone who has qualitative skills, one of your interview questions will probably need a qualitative answer.

- If internal, talk to as many team members as possible to get an idea of their perspectives on the open position. If the position is external, find people who work or have worked at the company to give insight that could be beneficial.

- Thoroughly review the skills needed to be successful in the position and create a skills matrix; align your history to the skills needed. The skills matrix is a document you can use to match your skills to what's needed. List the needs of the position from the job posting (for example: leadership, team building, financial acumen, etc.) in columns across the top. In the columns down the side of the page, list your most impactful stories (history). Using a grid, place check marks in the boxes where your stories and their needs meet. This allows you to see areas where your skills and history match. This matrix can be used as examples to demonstrate your competencies.

- Do not only think about how you will answer certain questions; it is critical to actually **practice**. Practice looking in the mirror and answering the questions out loud. This prep work will help you clarify your thoughts and make you more comfortable during the interview. Use your cell phone to record yourself. Listen to the playback so you can hear where adjustments may be needed.

Before the interview: Get your head in the right place

- Get to the interview location early. You do not want to start off with the negative energy of being tardy
- Eat a good breakfast or lunch (based on the time of your interview)
- Relax your mind before the interview (try meditation)
- Do not schedule meetings or hard tasks before your interview
- Do not cram for the interview right before your interview

Execute interview preparation (virtual or in-person)

- Know the information. Ensure you have talking points and have practiced what you are going to say and how you are going to say it.
- Do not sound like a script. Practice but be natural.
- Anticipate questions
- Do not include things in your presentation you do not understand or know the details. Once I assisted someone with a presentation; they decided to use a concept I suggested in their presentation; however, they did not understand it well enough to answer more than the basic definition. If you take advise and use concepts from others, think about how you would use the concept within your role and whether you fully understand it. You can get help with your presentation but you need to make it yours, not someone else's ideas.

Dress for the interview

- Hair groomed, nails neat and, if in-person, shoes shined.
- For females, have nails manicured and tastefully polished and an appropriate length.

- Belt should match shoes.
- Blue, black and gray are the colors for traditional suits. Other colors can be worn; however, refrain from wearing trendy colors.

<u>More interview tips</u>

- If in person, bring copies of your resume and any item(s) relevant to your experience and/or skills.
- If virtual, email a PDF of your resume and a copy of item(s) to validate your experience and/or skills prior to the interview.
- If you are planning to have show- and-tell information, please ensure it is in a professional style presentation package.
- Be prepared to articulate why you are the best candidate, specifically in your closing
- Ask For The Job!

Some of these tips sound like common sense but I have found they are often overlooked. I have had many interviews over the course of my career. Some of the positions I received and others I did not, but regardless I always asked for feedback. Some companies are not at liberty to provide feedback to external candidates but if you are interviewing internally, requesting feedback is acceptable.

Once, I interviewed for an executive position - VP of Technology - with a major sports team. I had interviews with six different leaders and used the above techniques within the six sessions. At the end of each, I asked for feedback. I also asked if there was information I needed for the next interview. Other interviews I have had consisted of panels; this is more common in corporate America. Depending on the company's hiring practices, you may have additional types of interviews. In either case, the tips above are helpful and, if applied, could make a huge difference.

Exercise #8: INTERVIEW PRACTICE

Practicing for an interview can seem intimidating and stressful. As you practice your presentation or interview answers, record yourself. After you listen to your recording, evaluate your performance by answering the questions provided below. You may use this exercise template each time you interview. The goal is to have crisp, well prepared answers to potential questions related to your interview or presentation.

Example: Interview Practice Exercise

Things to watch/listen for in your recording:	Critiquing your answer from listening to your recording:
How long was my response? If there was a time limit given to a presentation topic, are you within the time?	Question response was 5 minutes. I rambled thus it was too long. OR Presentation was 5 minutes but I was allotted 10 minutes. I need to add more valuable information. I have 5 slides and that's enough for 10 minutes.
Did the response, answer the question or the presentation topic question? You may have a spouse, friend, or peer critic this.	My response answered the question but there was too much detail so it was too long. OR I'm not sure if I answered the presentation question. I might need to get a second opinion.
How many times did I say "ahh" while I was thinking of my response?	I said "ahh" 10 times in 5 minutes when answering the question. I will work on that. OR I was so nervous recording the presentation, I said "ahh" 26 times in 10 minutes. I will work on that.
Was my response or delivery of the presentation succinct?	No, question response was too long, not succinct. OR Yes, presentation was too succinct. Need more vital information.

INSTRUCTIONS: Complete the chart below once you have recorded and listened to (or watched if video) your recording.

Interview Practice Exercise Worksheet

Questions to listen for in my recording	Critique your answer from listening
How long was my response? If there was a time limit given to a presentation topic, are you within the time?	
Did the response, answer the question or the presentation topic question?	
How many times did I say "ahh" while I was thinking of my response?	
Was my response or delivery of the presentation succinct?	

Volunteering for Extra or "Stretch" Assignments

Earlier in the chapter, I briefly mentioned volunteering for extra assignments or community projects but I think the topic deservers a deeper dive. In this section, I will share additional insight about volunteering, why it is important and how it can benefit you and your company. Volunteering has been a way for me to sharpen my skills, learn new skills, and share my passion with the community.

In 2019, I was asked to sit on the Board of the Jacksonville State University (JSU) Black Alumni Chapter as the Vice President of Scholarships. The Board had been around for a while but not very active. The new president needed dedicated people to help resurrect the Chapter. After weeks of thinking about it and discussing with my family, I decided to volunteer. The Vice President of Scholarships was one of the more challenging roles on the Board because it involved engaging people and making them comfortable enough to donate. Since no one could recall the Chapter previously awarding scholarships, this was going to be a new venture for everyone.

After almost a year of marketing and communication, we were able to get people excited about helping the scholarship team reach their goals. We raised enough money to award over $40K in annual scholarships over a four-year period, which was phenomenal. We also created enough momentum to start an endowment fund with $30K seed money. What a difference a volunteer team can make!

Because of the work that was done on the smaller chapter alumni board, I was named JSU 2020 Alumna of the Year and asked to volunteer for the JSU Foundation Board. This board is directly under the Board of Trustees, and is responsible for some of the operations of the University and millions of donation dollars.

The above is one example of community involvement and how you could potentially be recognized for your expertise and efforts. My volunteerism for this project was also recognized by my work organization. I received accolades from many within the company and I flexed another skill set that my leadership noticed and later utilized. In this role, I was able to use marketing skills to develop my fundraising skills in a less risky environment. I learned how to connect with others more deeply via social media and online marketing. I also gained a deeper understanding of storytelling which helped me tremendously in my business career. Below are some additional benefits of volunteering.

The Benefits of Volunteering

We all have a lot on our to-do lists, but to be in the game we sometimes have to do a bit extra. Volunteering is one of the tactics I found helpful. I hope you can tell, I am passionate about community service and helping others so volunteering comes natural for me. You are the one who knows yourself the best; find a place where you want to contribute, an area you are passionate about and volunteer. Most senior leaders are on Boards and are involved in community activities so volunteering is a wonderful way to open doors to access these leaders. Some key benefits of volunteering include those listed below:

Benefits of Volunteering	Comments
Meeting new leaders	You never know who you might meet while volunteering and serving the community.
Gaining new skills	Think of this assignment as a new opportunity to explore fresh territory and gain additional skills. Think about it as a non-threatening way to shore up skills you may need for your individual development plan.
Helping customers, the community, and the company	Making a positive impact
Soaring your morale and sense of accomplishment and engagement.	We all need a morale booster every now and then

Exercise #9: VOLUNTEER GUIDE TO SUCCESS

INSTRUCTIONS: Volunteer for a new assignment and use the below chart as a guide to success. Input your comments as you go through the volunteer process.

Guidance	Comments	Your thoughts or Comments
Make the project or initiative yours	Bring innovative ideas to the table. Think about things in a way that no one else does	
Brainstorm the project or initiative with people you trust	Put your thoughts together and develop well thought out plans	
Think through executive-level questions that may be asked	List the questions with your answers so they sound crisp and well thought through	
Think about what skills you will enhance from the volunteer assignment	Hopefully, the skills you are enhancing are ones from your development plan you created earlier	

I now take on new assignments as challenges and opportunities in order to put my fingerprint on projects and programs that need my way of thinking and special touch. I use special assignments as developmental or learning opportunities.

It may be a good idea to volunteer for high profile, high visibility opportunities, but it should also be something you are passionate about. Working at something you care about does not feel like work. Step up and volunteer for projects that

- will help you to stand out
- may lead to other opportunities
- help you learn and grow

In my earlier example with the JSU Board, I had no idea I was being considered for the Foundation Board while I served as VP of Scholarships. I was doing what I loved; helping students be successful by getting an education.

If you are presented with a once in a lifetime opportunity, make time for it. If you are being exposed to a new area, embrace it. It is important to remember that all volunteer efforts do not lead to something greater. If it does not, feel good about helping others.

CASE STUDY #7: VOLUNTEERING IN ACTION

I love working with non-profit organizations. When I first became a manager, I came across a volunteer opportunity to lead an initiative for the department. When leadership asked, "Who wants to take on the leadership for the project this year?," the room was silent for a few seconds. I raised my hand; I wanted the opportunity to show what I could do. However, keep in mind before you volunteer, evaluate the opportunity and decide if it is something want to and can do.

I put together a small team of diverse minds and we came up with a plan and goals for a department of over a 100 people. I reviewed the plan with the executives and we started to execute. The events were innovative, new, and highly successful; our department was the only one to reap all the internal incentives for participating that year and was a guideline for future events.

I also had an opportunity to present to the entire department at a meeting where senior leadership attended; it was awesome! Had I not volunteered, I would not have gained visibility and demonstrated my business skills while working on a corporate charity project.

Change your thinking about taking on extra assignments. If you have the capacity, show your organization what you can do. Take the assignment and make it your own. Create the strategy, execute your vision, and update the executives along the way. If nothing else, they will know your name and think of you when other assignments come along. Before you know it, you are on your way. One of my mentors once told me "take on the assignments that no one else wants," do a good job, and you will soar. I give you the same advice.

EXERCISE #10 – VOLUNTEERING MISSED OPPORTUNITIES

INSTRUCTIONS: List the times you turned down or did not volunteer for an extra/side assignment for any reason.

1. _____

2. _____

3. _____

4. _____

Review your list above, put a star on those that could have been an opportunity for you to shine or make a connection with a power professional. Do not let another opportunity pass you by.

Note any relationships you have built below from volunteering. I am holding you accountable. You cannot just read this information; you must act.

INSTRUCTIONS: Think about previous volunteer activities. List any new relationships that resulted from volunteering.

1. _____

2. _____

3. _____

EXERCISE #11 – REFLECTIVE JOURNALING EXERCISE

INSTRUCTIONS: Take a moment to journal about your experience when you said "YES" to a volunteer project/activity. What new skillset did you acquire? How will you use those skillsets going forward? What current skillsets did you sharpen? How will you nurture the new relationships built?

_____

_____

_____

_____

_____

_____

_____

_____

_____

_____

_____

_____

_____

Encouraging Volunteerism as a Leader

If you are a leader in a company and you do not have an employee volunteer program, here are a few reasons why a program would be beneficial for the business and the employee.

- Recruiting and hiring the best talent is what every company wants. Potential employees, especially GenZer's, are very in tune with community and work volunteer programs. Companies should highlight opportunities and efforts which will allow potential employees to get a sense of the company's ideals, mission, and vision. At one point in my career, I was at a crossroad and changed companies frequently; three companies in three years. The companies did enough to get me in the door but once I started, I did not feel a connection to the company. After searching, I eventually found a company where I stayed over 25 years because I was connected to the values of the company. They had a corporate culture I identified with and retained me for most of my career.
- The second benefit is employee retention. When team members have pride in the work that is being done by the company, retention is improved. When good employees stay at a company there is a long-term benefit around the cost savings associated with recruiting and hiring new employees.
- The third benefit is skill development. Volunteer programs are safe spaces and effective ways to help employees develop skills that will in turn benefit their job performance.

Companies focused on social responsibility are more likely to attract top talent. When employees volunteer for initiatives they are enthusiastic about, they will give it their all. If employees have not found their passion, you can help them by being an example. When you let team members see your heart, you model the way. Volunteering can show your drive for excellence and a commitment to making a difference. Connect the values you are passionate about to the values of the company. When you have an authentic connection, you build trust with your team. As I shared earlier, my values connected with my companies values thus I stayed over 25 years.

Ask each team member what they are excited about and listen to their answer. Look for opportunities where they can thrive. Once in a one-on-one with my leader, I was asked the question, "Cheryl, what do you like to do? What are you passionate about?" If you cannot answer this question, you need to self-reflect and try to determine where your enthusiasm lies. My answer at the time was that I had passion for:

- problem solving
- creating new products and services
- people initiatives
- international business

He listened and noted my responses. Later I was presented with an opportunity to take a position that allowed me to lead a department in some of the areas I was excited about. After I conquered the first assignment, he moved me to another where there were other passion areas for me. I was thriving! I was helping the company and doing things I loved that were challenging and fulfilling.

While flourishing in the second role, I was promoted to a position that had one area I was enthusiastic about. I grew my organization into an area where I had several departments which helped me continue to be creative and excited. Sometimes we have to create our ideal job by taking on new responsibilities. Find the work you LOVE and do it! If you are doing what you love, the pay and/or accolades will follow.

CASE STUDY #8: PASSION IN ACTION

I know a prominent real estate attorney at Regency Title and Escrow in Memphis, Tennessee. He loves people; he loves talking to people and sees himself as the final step to people obtaining the American dream of home ownership. I often tell him he can talk to a total stranger and immediately find a connection. He has the gift of making people feel comfortable and garnering trust. Closing loans is not a job for him; he often says he gets paid for doing what he loves and that is helping people realize their home ownership dream. Agents and lending institutions love and trust him and his staff which is validated in their repeat business. Customers love and trust him which is validated by the cakes and Christmas gifts he receives each year. When you are passionate about something it shows. You don't have to talk about it or shout it from the rooftops, it automatically bleeds through in your natural actions. When you love the work you do, you thrive.

This chapter has covered a lot of information; thus you may want to read it more than once. The major points I'd like you to remember are listed below.

MAJOR POINTS TO REMEMBER FROM THIS CHAPTER:

Support of your immediate manager is important
If you do not have your immediate managers support, work to get it
One of the ways to try and get the support you need is to volunteer for extra work assignments or community assignments to gain additional experience and skills
If you cannot change the perception, you may need to move to a new area
If you need to interview to change areas, review the interview techniques

EXERCISE #12 – REFLECTIVE JOURNALING EXERCISE

INSTRUCTIONS: Think about this chapter. Take a few minutes to journal your most important learnings from this chapter and any actions you will take.

LEARNINGS: _____

_____

_____

_____

_____

_____

_____

ACTIONS: _____

_____

_____

_____

_____

_____

_____

CHAPTER 5

YOUR WORKPLACE PERCEPTION AND YOUR WORKPLACE CULTURE

"Perception is reality," is a saying I am sure you may have heard. Although it may not be 100% true, if other people's perception of you is not what you want, ask yourself the question, "Is there something I'm doing to give them this perception?"

Years ago, I surveyed a few co-workers and asked them to share their workplace perception of me. The results were:

- I was quietly competitive
- I was excellent at execution
- A great team builder

When I asked my immediate family the same question, they said:

- I was bossy
- I took over to ensure things were done according to my standards
- A great organizer

In thinking about the difference in perception, I questioned, "Am I being my authentic self at work?" My workplace perception was described in this manner because I tried not to appear bossy; therefore, I came across as quiet. I had taken the word bossy as a negative instead of looking at it as a positive and channeling it in the right way at the right time. Yes, channeling your energy correctly is work but it can be done. If there is a negative or incorrect perception of you in your workplace, I have detailed a few ideas that may help.

CASE STUDY #9: PLEASE READ THE CASE STUDY TO GAIN WORPLACE PERCEPTION INSIGHT

I attended a conference and heard someone say that a way to overcome negative perceptions or incorrect perceptions is to find two or three words that you want people to say when they talk about you. For example, if you want your boss to have confidence in you as a leader, you may say something like: "Mason did an excellent job today. I'm so proud of him. You know my new leadership approach with Mason is really working." This will show your mentoring and leadership skills. With the right tactics, it is very possible that perceptions may change. Please note, this is just one example and this tactic is a way to share the actual work you are doing in a way the leadership team can see your part in it.

Another example is if you want people to think you are analytical, you can say, "I received the data and analyzed it with Mason. Although it was a long meeting, I believe I helped him with his analytical thought process. And together we were able to create a great work product." You don't want to go overboard but you do want to help change your perception while you are being your authentic self. The above examples may sound a bit like self-promotion and, to some extent, it might be. But it is a valuable tool to share the work of yourself and your team if you are in a leadership position. The below information sheds some light on self-promotion.

Self-promotion – Women vs. Men Insight

Self-promotion is showing your value through results, facts, and differentiation. In a *Harvard Business Review* article titled "Why Don't Women Self-Promote as Much as Men?," it shared a large gender gap as it relates to self-promotion. What they found was that men engaged in substantially more self-promotion than women. Some say that women have been conditioned to take a back seat to wait to be recognized. Seems women are much more comfortable doing the work. For example, despite the fact that men and women performed equally well in the study, men rated themselves an average of 61 out of 100 while women only rated themselves a 46 out of 100. What drove this difference in self-promotion? It was validated that women were under confident about their performance and men were overconfident."[1]

It seems evident that women don't prefer to self-promote and often cannot see themselves doing it. Women sometimes feel guilty about saying how good they are. It doesn't seem natural. But men seem to do it all the time and sometimes for the smallest things. You should appropriately tell your leadership team the value you are bringing to their organization. Don't assume they know. If you get into the habit of sharing accomplishments and updates about what you do, it won't seem like you are self-promoting but just updating. Take it upon yourself to do it even if it's not asked for. Try it once a month for six months and see if you are perceived differently. There are many books and studies you can research on the internet to get a better understanding of this concept. Look for topics that discuss self-promotion, strategy, and personal branding.

Self-promotion takes practice. When you are self-promoting you must be sincere, talk about others and the role they played, and don't be dismissive about your accomplishments. Why self-promote? People are busy, priorities shift, technology and the pandemic have changed how we work. As high performing individuals, we must not be overlooked. Here are a few things for women to think about related to self-promotion:

- You are an inspiration - your career self-promotion motivates others. When you get outside of your comfort zone and talk about yourself, you learn how to inspire others
- Frame your achievements in terms of impact - it's really about the impact to the department or the company. Learn to summarize succinctly.
- Tell your story and give yourself the credit you deserve - your story is your story, don't be so critical, ease up, don't minimize your accomplishments
- Don't keep your successes to yourself. Tell others. You can attract new opportunities by sharing your success in your current opportunities
- Don't listen to negative people. Career self-promotion is sometime difficult and may not seem natural, but it is a skill worth developing
- Women who self-promote or make their accomplishments visible had greater career satisfaction and are more likely to attract sponsors

- Promote and advocate for other women
- Build an interesting and compelling story about your accomplishments. Don't just state a bunch of statistics. Weave the successes into a story that is entertaining and informative
- Highlight results with enthusiasm opposed to being matter of fact
- Show self-confidence by accepting compliments graciously

When self-promoting, use language such as, "My team did an exceptional job on this special project. I am thankful to lead such a results-oriented team." Don't use language like this, "I was brought on to lead the special project and led the team to do an exceptional job." The first example sounds more humble and sincere than the second.

Other ways you can self-promote is to be insightful when you're having conversations. Take appropriate opportunities to share prior achievements and successes or create opportunities for other people or ask your advocates to promote your work. Think through various ideas and determine what works best for you. Women are known to carry the additional burden of battling ingrained social stereotypes that prescribe female modesty. The role of women in the workplace is changing and the disparity may be lessening. There is beauty in finding the balance between demonstrating your skills and boasting about them. It can be difficult to find the balance but getting it right can open doors to promotions, new clients or other opportunities. Again, be open, authentic and modest.

Self-promotion - Workplace

In talking to those who work at various companies about the self-promotion concept, I've found it is easier to bring the theory to life through examples which a few are shared above. I'd like to share three specific workplace situations where you can practice self-promotion.

1st WORKPLACE SELF PROMOTION EXAMPLE

I was able to experience a manager who sent emails when his team reached milestones within major projects. After studying him for about a year, I realized that when the milestones were really significant he emailed the highest levels of management to share the success. In the background, his name and his team were being remembered because of this small gesture. He was branding his team and himself. He was getting his name out in the internal marketplace. For this manager, it was a win/win. After a year or so of this behavior (and I'm sure significant work), this manager was promoted. All situations are different, this tactic alone probably won't get you promoted but it is a tool you can use to help with visibility.

2nd WORKPLACE SELF PROMOTION EXAMPLE

Another way to get corporate visibility is to insert time appropriate leadership updates. Important projects need executive sponsors and executive updates. When leading a project ensure there are regularly scheduled email, zoom or in-person updates to leadership. Good project managers or scrum masters have dashboards or some mechanism to use for updating everyone that needs to know. Leaders want to know what's going on with major projects. Don't keep them guessing. It should bother you when your leadership sends you an email asking how the project is going. Be proactive, gain confidence, get visibility, and self-promote by sharing regular updates.

NOTE: YOU must understand when you've done enough self-promotion. Self-promoting too much can be as bad as not self-promoting at all. Self-promotion when you don't have facts and results can be destructive. Self-promoting to get general attention is a bad idea.

3rd WORKPLACE SELF PROMOTION EXAMPLE

The last example I will share is one of a high performing manager I once had the privilege to lead. At the beginning of each year we created her annual objectives. We reviewed them quarterly to see if we were on track. In addition, at the end of the year she would create a document to share all the impressive results she delivered to the company in relation to her objectives. She was self-promoting in a way that was based on our collective objectives with facts and results. I used that same information to share with my leadership to advocate on her behalf. This helped me justify bonus' and extra recognition for her. It also made it very easy for me to do her annual performance review.

There are many ways to self-promote, find the one that makes sense to you, feels natural to you, and allows you to be true to yourself. To not self-promote is not really an option. If you don't self-promote you may be thinking shortsighted and negative thoughts like the ones below:

- "My accomplishments should speak for themselves." Don't sit in your cubicle like I did early on and just work. You need a good work product but you must share your accomplishments.
- "I don't want to brag." If done right, you aren't bragging; you are sharing the success of your team and yourself.
- "My boss is busy and don't have time to hear me talk about myself." Your boss should have time to hear about accomplishments that benefit his/her department.
- "Team players don't take credit." Learn to step into the spotlight. If you are a major player on the team, accept the accolades.
- "Everyone is good on the team but I feel inadequate. I can't possibly self-promote." Get a mentor or someone to give you real feedback about your performance. If your thoughts are valid, change things. If your thoughts are not valid, learn to self-promote.

CASE STUDY #10: PLEASE READ THE CASE STUDY TO GAIN INSIGHT ON HOW TO THINK MORE POSITIVELY

During the Summer 2022 Intern Program at the company I worked, one of the interns came to me and was very concerned about her workplace perception. The Program divided the interns into groups with typically four in a group. This intern was concerned because she thought she was being perceived as not pulling her weight. She was a sophomore in college and the other three interns were getting their master's degree. I talked with her about her contributions to the group; I, in turn, talked with her team members about their perception of her in the group. They thought she was doing a really good job as their "scrum master" and contributing to the development (coding the UI or User Interface) of the project in ways that they found valuable. She was thinking negative thoughts and not giving herself credit for the value she brought to the team.

> You should not over inflate your work but at the same time you must give yourself credit when you do good work. One must have a balance. I can understand her perspective, especially as an intern. You don't really know how you are doing unless you are receiving feedback.

As leaders, we have the responsibility to give the gift of feedback to our team members. Good leaders learn to give actionable feedback. Whether they are just starting out in the workforce or if they've been in corporate for years, actionable feedback helps team members continue to grow and it also says, "I'm interested in you and your professional growth."

EXERCISE #13: HOW WOULD YOU LIKE TO BE PRECEIVED AT WORK?

INSTRUCTIONS: List three characteristics that describe how you would like to be perceived. Below are example words to consider as characteristics to get you started.

1. _____

2. _____

3. _____

EXAMPLE WORDS:

Exceptional Leader	Finance Expert	Marketing Expert	Smart
Strong Mentor	Decision Maker	Outgoing	Entertainer

CASE STUDY #11: PLEASE READ THE PERCEPTION CASE STUDY LIFE APPLICATION

I was on a plane coming from a training session and the flight attendants were preparing for take-off. There was one flight attendant who saw a man with a big bag under his chair and she said in a very mean tone, "Oh no that won't work; that bag can't be under the seat. You're going to have to put it up or check it!" She did not use a friendly tone or say, "Excuse me sir." On the same flight this same attendant saw someone with their cell phone out. She said, "No cell phones!" as she continued to walk through the isle. The person said "Excuse me Miss, excuse me." She turned around and he said "I turned my radio off so my phone isn't transmitting. I'm playing solitaire. She said "No cell phones period." She was very nasty in every situation when she really didn't have to be. She was being perceived by most on the plane as being over the top. Sometimes we may say or do something that comes across in a different way from what we intended. I'm sure she thought she was just doing her job or maybe she was having a bad day but we should be very cognizant of the messages we are delivering.

Important Perception Note: One other item to consider when thinking through your workplace perception is how do you present your work? I worked with an executive coach over the years and he helped me to understand that perception matters even on paper. Do you present all **facts** and **substance** or do you present **facts and substance** with **sizzle**? When people think about how they present themselves, they may question whether their outfits are attractive or are they groomed appropriately. Analysis/facts and substance is necessary, but you should again present your work, i.e. milestones, emails, and presentations with sizzle. Sizzle means having the correct positioning, knowing your target audience, connecting the right strategies with the appropriate colors and graphics. Market your work and yourself. Understand what's important to the audience and arrange the information in a way that it is inviting and easy to read. Not all charts and tables. Pictures are truly sometimes worth more than words.

Your Workplace Culture

The culture of your company should be contemplated when thinking about your workplace perception. Sometimes your workplace perception is not what you want it to be because you don't understand the culture of the company. Understanding how the department and the company works is almost as important as knowing how to do your job. If the culture is one that makes decisions in "the meeting before the meeting," you cannot expect to change that. If you come to the meeting expecting to have a discussion to make a decision, you will have missed it. In the Broadway play "Hamilton," there is a scene that talks about "being in the room when it happens." You will need to be invited to the "meeting before the meeting" so you can be in the room when things happen. Better yet, you set up the "meeting before the meeting," align with who you need to align with and you are ready. The bottom line is in order to play the game, you need to know the rules. Understanding the culture of the organization is part of understanding the rules. Once you understand the rules you will have a better chance to exhibit your intended perception.

A healthy culture within a company can help make team members feel connected, safe and able to share their true ideas and perspectives. Organizations with a supportive culture have invested in developing leaders who lead their teams with respect and encouragement. When employees feel removed and do not understand how their work contributes to the overall success of the company, a disconnect occurs. It is up to you to seek information for understanding the company's culture and how all of it works in unison. It is up to the leadership to build a culture of trust, inclusiveness, openness, and volunteerism.

I've mentioned the word trust a few times throughout this book. The Merriam Webster dictionary defines trust as "assured reliance on the character, ability, strength or truth of someone or something."

Having trust in the workplace among coworkers can have the following effects:

Enhances teamwork, collaboration, and creativity	Allows decision making to become easier
Increases employee engagement	Improves organizational alignment
Lowers resistance to change	Lowers stress in team members
Reduces turnover	Helps employees feel secure in their jobs

Not only is trust needed among coworkers, but leaders must also build trust with their teams. When teams feel secure with leaders and how they operate, they believe their best interest and the company's best interest are top of mind.

Leaders must be authentic, listen, learn, and act. Good leaders have a robust listening framework to make sure all voices are heard and turn those insights to action. When people trust leaders to listen and act, they expect to be updated on progress. The way I've brought this concept to life with my teams is by having quarterly listening circles.

Listening circles allow me to solicit feedback that can be acted on. It also gives me the opportunity to encourage, inspire, and show appreciation to team members in an intimate setting. I ask my team ahead of time for questions or topics they would like to discuss prior to the meeting. I do this because I want to have an opportunity to research and be prepared with as much information as possible for the discussion.

We come together in-person or via zoom with a mostly free form agenda. I want my team to know I am open and listening to them. I take notes and share them, along with action items, with my direct leadership team and track the action. Actions that I need to tackle at my level, I work on them.

My output is to give updates in quarterly town halls. Town halls are when I bring my entire team together in person and/or zoom to hear company updates and pertinent business and industry information. In addition, the company, I worked for at the time, had annual employee surveys where we collectively heard from our entire body of team members. A similar action plan is created and actions officially tracked.

Below is a high-level example of a leadership action plan:

High Level Plan	Date to be implemented
Create an atmosphere of growth and learning • Protect the IP sprint within the PI for learning • Select a book for a book club discussion	• End of fiscal year • December 2022
Build an atmosphere of trust and accountability • Managers to implement monthly one-on-one meetings with team members • Give clear and specific directions with success consequences and coaching sessions	• July 2022 • ASAP
Share the "why" behind major decisions • Share within town halls and/or other departmental meetings	• Start the beginning of the fiscal year

It is said that a happy employee equals a productive employee. I agree because I am at my best when working with a company where I trust the leadership, my peers, and my team. That is an ideal situation; however, it takes time for team members to develop a level of trust. Authenticity is a key factor to gaining trust. After you take a look at the case studies below, we will dig a bit deeper into the topic of authenticity.

CASE STUDY #12: PLEASE READ THE CASE STUDY ABOUT TEAMMEMBER TRUST

I had a low trust team member, who wasn't performing as needed, with a negative attitude which was permeating to others on the team. He was upset because he had been reorganized to a team where he had to learn a new skill set. He was resistant to change and felt he had been unjustly moved and shared this anyone who would listen. His manager shared the situation with me and we put together a plan to help new team members learn skills necessary to be successful. We also assigned him a mentor who had been doing the same job on another team, empowering him to bring any transferable best practices to make our work group operate more smoothly. The manager had a weekly check-in meeting with this team member and I set up a monthly check-in meeting to reinforce and empower the team member. Over time, the manager, the mentor, and I were able to build a trusting relationship with this team member and turn them around. It wasn't instant; it took 8-12 months. The team member had to see us exhibiting what we said and supporting him through his learning curve. Eventually he got to the point where he was secure in his new position, understood why he was reorganized, and how his lack of effort contributed to previous low performance. It is not always that team members have an "aha" moment, but it's always exciting as a leader when they do.

I had another scenario where a team member applied for a new position, interviewed, and got the job. He worked in the new position for about six weeks and discovered he really didn't thoroughly read the job description and the job wasn't what he wanted. In this instance, the team member came to me directly and was frantic because he was in the wrong job. He trusted me to help him correct the situation, which I did by working with his manager to create a plan to move the team member into a position where he could be successful. How did we do this?

- We looked within the immediate workgroup to see if a rotation was available on a more suitable team
- The manager and I worked across our peer levels to see if anyone had a need for his skillset and the kind of projects he wanted to contribute to
- We also helped him look for positions internal to the company via the company intranet

We found a rotation opportunity on another team within my organization. The team member worked in my group for another two years because he trusted us as leaders, he felt included, and valued.

BE AUTHENTIC

Authenticity is key to building trust and is how we express who we are, and an alignment between how we feel and what we show. When you are inauthentic or more worried about style and impression over substance and action, you may be perceived as fake or insincere. I have found that being open, asking questions, and telling my personal stories of success and failure help me connect and build rapport as a leader.

Through my journey, I learned to be structured and professional; that is really who I am. However, in the past, I have been seen as too "buttoned up" and not authentic. I say to you, if that is who you are, be who you are. Stay true to your core values. Once people got to know me, they realize this is just how I operate; it's a part of my formal personality and I am who I am.

When we lose touch with our own values and become so focused on other people's opinions and priorities, we can be perceived as insincere. The best way to maintain the kind of presence that feels authentic to yourself and others is to create the right balance between introspection and input. Take the opportunity to revisit who you are, what matters to you, and what you hope to achieve.

In my twenties, as I continued to learn who I was, my strengths and weaknesses, my beliefs, goals, and dreams, I found I had become what I thought I needed to be to survive in corporate America. I felt like I needed to be perfect for my parents, my husband, my children, my brothers, and my co-workers. I carried a huge weight on my shoulders that no one placed there except me. I cared deeply about what others thought of me, and I really didn't think I deserved to be where I was. I was in my spot, the place I was supposed to be, in my chair at the table but still felt I was not enough. I hid part of myself. People used to tell me in one-on-one conversations, "You are so funny. I never would have thought that from the meetings we are in together. You are usually always so serious."

I've had many people pour into me from a mentoring perspective. One session I remember vividly was with a senior leader named Tracci. She said, "You are here for a reason. It's not just about a job. Sit in your seat because no one can sit in it but you. When you are not in your seat, giving your perspective from your point of view you are not giving the company or your team members what they need. We are depending on you."

That was a powerful message to me and a wakeup call. I had a job to do and I was selected to be in that position that needed the "unique" me. When I began to understand myself, my beliefs, my passions, I began to walk in my truth; I gave myself permission to be me and started to appreciate the journey that is uniquely mine.

In one of the episodes of the TV series, *How to Get Away with Murder*, the star character Annalise Keating took off her wig, eyelashes and makeup so we could see the "real" her; no filter with all her flaws and beauty. That's what we must do. Take it all off, lay it on the table, and figure out how to be the best You. The work must be done to determine who you are, otherwise, you might feel like an imposter and that can be draining.

Before my self-reflective journey, I would come home from work and tell my kids, "Mommy needs 10 minutes." I needed that time to change my face if you will. Take off my wig, lashes, and makeup like Annalise so I could be myself.

When you know who you are, there is a "balanced" you that shows up at work and home. You don't have to change your "face" from one to the other. Yes, you will probably be more relaxed outside of work but you shouldn't be a totally different person. Once I did the work, I showed up to work as ME!

I show my funny side by making jokes, when appropriate. But I also share my journey with whomever is interested. Much of effective leadership is about educating through our own journeys. Our successes and failures show we are human and have the ability to analyze and learn from our experiences. By sharing our own narratives, we give permission for others to do the same.

People thrive when they are authentic, working in their purpose and passion. They bring their whole person to the workplace, to the conversation, to the project, and to the community. We are all diverse and have different journeys and can bring a unique perspective to every situation.

Exercise #14: ARE YOU AUTHENTIC?

INSTRUCTIONS: Be honest and take time to answer the two questions below. Answer either yes or no. Once you have completed part 1, reflect and journal in part 2.

<u>Part 1</u> – Answer yes or no

1. **Are you your authentic self?**
2. **Are you being true to yourself?**

<u>Part 2</u> - **If your answer is no to either of the questions above, write down in the space below the roadblocks that prevent you from being your true, authentic self at work.**

_____

_____

_____

_____

If you aren't being perceived as authentic you might

- constantly feel misunderstood
- feel like the victim
- feel like you are wearing a mask (like you have to be perfect or impress others)
- over analyze your ideas and thoughts (while you shouldn't blurt out everything that comes to mind, you shouldn't sit quietly, overanalyzing if you should share or not)
- feel like you are always letting yourself and others down (your small milestones are a really big deal to someone else. Yes, set the bar high but if you get almost there, celebrate, and keep pressing forward)

Do the work to understand what's going on so you can learn and grow. If you do the work, it's therapeutic and can be life changing. You will be glad you did!

Authentic leadership feeds into the company culture. If companies and leaders are not interested in creating a culture of inclusiveness, trust, authenticity, and honesty, this should send up a red flag. A great culture not only helps to get new employees, but it also helps to retain them. You must understand the culture and the environment to successfully maneuver within it.

CHAPTER 6

BE FLEXIBLE & THINK THOUGH YOUR REACTIONS WITH COURAGE

The Lesson of Flexibility

The lesson of being flexible is dear to me because it was one that required practice. I am a planner and believed I was flexible until I found out that I was not. My experiences may be unique to me but hopefully you will be able to relate.

I had worked several days on a presentation I thought was perfect. After reviewing and triple checking the data, I was confident and presented it to my manager as a preview. He was not impressed. He moved data, changed verbiage, graphics, and almost everything else I had done. In my opinion, the information was the same so I could not understand why it was so important to have the information be presented in the way he wanted. I was upset and left the meeting deflated.

I went home, regrouped, thought about the changes, reformatted the information, and shared it again. Although, he was pleased, I still felt disheartened. I asked him why the changes were needed and while I heard his explanation, I still was not receptive.

A few months later, I went to an executive communications class where the instructor presented information that validated what my boss stated months earlier. The original presentation I put together was logical but did not consider my audience. I only thought of details and data I wanted to share, no sizzle. If I had been flexible and open to what my boss had said, I would have learned the art of adding sizzle to my work and understanding my audience much sooner.

We should have an open mind and be receptive for continued growth and development. A closed mindset will never learn because it is not flexible. A flexible mindset has positive attributes, as shared below:

Positivity	Digest information and situations, seeking positive learning opportunities. Have a love of learning. See the glass half full. Positivity will improve career success
Resilient	Be able to withstand change or recover quickly. Do not take months to recover or understand. We have to bend and be flexible
Thrive through obstacles	Instead of viewing obstacles as challenges, think of them as problems to solve or opportunities. Challenges are seen as negatives but can be viewed as something to overcome.

Being flexible is about rolling with the punches and taking things as they come. Have you ever heard the saying, "When life gives you lemons, make lemonade?" You need to be able to determine when you have lemons and what is your recipe for lemonade.

In spring 2020, I was a university commencement speaker and spoke about making lemonade out of lemons. I shared this with the graduating class.

> *"No matter what city you grew up in, if you had a two-parent or a single-parent home or if you lived in an apartment, the projects, or a home, you now have a bachelor's degree which is an ingredient to begin making your special lemonade. It's up to you to take the ingredients you were given and make something happen."*

Each one of us, with our individual, unique ingredients, will make different kinds of lemonade. They will not all taste the same but will still tastes good. There is a traditional recipe for lemonade; however, if we do not have the normal ingredients, we can improvise. That is where flexibility is important. You may not have regular sugar, but you might have artificial sweetener. You may not have real lemons, but you have lemon juice in a jar. Use what you have to create your own recipe.

All too often, we want everything to go according to plan and become distressed when things do not. Life happens causing us to look at alternatives or improvisions aside from what we are planning. We should always have contingency plans. If you are not a flexible person, it will be a challenge for you because you will need to deliberately create a plan B and C and, perhaps, change direction, depending on the circumstances.

Some people are naturally flexible and having a backup plan will be second nature, but for my inflexible people, please realize things do not always work out as planned. If you are falling apart when your plan or direction needs to change, it may be your actions and attitude causing a workplace perception you do not want. If you are a leader and not able to function in an environment of change, your team will see this and may take on the same attributes. As a leader you should always model positivity.

In one of my roles, I created a new customer incentive program for a transportation company and my key internal customer was the sales organization. Being familiar with the system from the ground up, I understood all the rules and guidelines, was aware of loopholes and the consequences of them.

Sales would frequently send an email or call me with their "special" customer scenarios. Once I acquired the art of flexibility, I became the queen of "going with the flow." I was able to consider the audience, what they were trying to accomplish, help them create solutions that dealt with their "special" customer scenario, and close the deal.

Everyone is not flexible and not able to deal with change. Change continues to be a constant with the multitude of diseases, viruses and technological advances in the world. As a leader, in order to help team members become more flexible, think through the following suggestions:

- Explain what is happening. Share the benefits to them as team members and the organization. Share the "why."
- Ensure team members feel secure. Try and create an environment of trust.
- Ensure long-term and short-term goals are clear. Communicate the purpose of the team and revisit them regularly.
- Encourage innovation. When people have a safe space to create, they find it easier to adapt to new things.

Reward and praise your team members when they show initiative and growth.

CASE STUDY #13: PERSONAL LIFE EXAMPLE ABOUT INFLEXIBILITY

One of my college mentees was a very process-oriented person and a good project manager. She prepared herself each night to ensure everything was in place and ready to go the next morning so that she could get to class on time. She got up in the morning, executing a routine that ended with caring for her dog. Heaven forbid, the toothpaste container was empty or there was not enough cereal in the box for her hearty breakfast, she would go nuts! By the same token, when she was in school and the teacher said, "Students we are not going to have our science test today", she would lose her mind because she'd studied and prepared for the test. She wanted to get it over with and check it off her list of things to do. Have you ever heard of someone who complains when a test was cancelled? Who does that? Do you know someone like this? We must be able to change course at any time with a positive attitude.

CASE STUDY #14: WORK LIFE EXAMPLE ABOUT INFLEXIBILITY:

I once had a team member who was particularly good at presentations, preparing, and delivering them. However, if you asked a question that was not in her script or speaker notes, she would lose her composure. She would look at the room with a blank stare, not having a clue how to answer because it was not in the script she had rehearsed. The script did not include a Q & A period so when questions were asked, she avoided answering which left the audience bewildered. In her mind she had done an outstanding job because her measurement of success was sticking to the script. Early on, I would step in answering questions and sharing examples with the audience. Once she heard the same questions a few times, she was able to add it to the script. However, in the business world, you must be able to think quickly. It is a good idea to walk through scenarios, with the help of others so you are prepared. You cannot display when you are annoyed, you must be flexible and "go with the flow." Remember, it is okay to say, "I'll check into that and get back to you."

Being flexible can be somewhat difficult but for the project managers reading this book, remember "slack" time is there for a reason. It allows the unexpected needs to be added to the plan, in case a task takes longer than scheduled.

Ask yourself, "Am I easy to do business with?" If the answer is no, you might not be as flexible as you think. The exercise below will help identify your flexibility.

EXERCISE #15 – ARE YOU FLEXIBLE?

Flexible Example

	I respond to changes in my plans by going with the flow
X	I respond to changes in my plans by becoming angry
	I respond to changes in my plans by quickly trying to create a new plan
	I am annoyed when my plans don't go my way
X	When I wake up in the morning if my routine is derailed, I am upset
	I go with the flow as long as my goals are accomplished
X	I think about the end goal opposed to each individual task
	When things don't go as planned, my initial thoughts are to focus on the **problem**
	When things don't go as planned, my initial thoughts are to focus on **solutions**
	When your performance is criticized by your superior, do you think you are being picked on and continue down the current path
3	*TOTAL*

INSTRUCTIONS: In the box below on the left side put a checkmark by every item that applies to you. Total your scores at the end and review the chart below to determine if you need to work on being more flexible.

Flexible Worksheet

	I respond to changes in my plans by going with the flow
	I respond to changes in my plans by becoming angry
	I respond to changes in my plans by quickly trying to create a new plan
	I am annoyed when my plans don't go my way
	When I wake up in the morning if my routine is derailed I am upset
	I go with the flow as long as my goals are accomplished
	I think about the end goal opposed to each individual task
	When things don't go as planned; my initial thoughts are to focus on the **problem**
	When things don't go as planned; my initial thoughts are to focus on **solutions**
	When your performance is criticized by your superior, do you think that you are being picked on and continue down the current path
	TOTAL

Score	Level of Flexibility
4 or above	Not very flexible (work on this area)
3 or below	Being flexible comes easy and should be used as an asset

Thoughtful & Courageous Reactions

When faced with difficulties in the work place, the ideal situation is to take time to let the information digest, think it through, find the positive, and then respond. Sometimes we do not have the luxury of time for the process so we must learn to have thoughtful reactions.

Keeping a cool head and open mind during a stressful meeting or conflict at the office goes a long way and may separate you from your coworkers. It can be stressful when you do not have the answer to a question or knowledge of information prior to a meeting; however, it is better to courageously respond with, "I'm not sure of the answer and I'll get back with you" or "That approach is interesting but I have the perspective of such and such", as opposed to reacting negatively. This state of mind may be difficult at first but it will become easier with practice.

I have learned a lot about myself through listening, self-reflection, and life experiences. Keep in mind, you can always reinvent yourself. You just need to get started.

A young man I know made some really bad decisions right out of high school. Before this, he was perceived as a good kid with good parents and family life. Because of his immature decision making, he ended up incarcerated for a year and a half. Once he was released, because of his faith and core beliefs, he had a sense of renewed values and a desire to do something different. He got a job so he could take care of his three children and wife, at the time. Fast forward 10 years later, he has four children, a grandchild and he is now the Chief Operating Officer (COO) of a multi-million-dollar company. It took hard work and time but he reinvented himself and is now reaping the benefits. Because of his background and amazing story, he speaks at conferences and venues where he can help others. He works in his church and community, feeds the homeless, and mentors other young men, encouraging them not to make the same mistakes he did. He also helps to employ those who have been in prison, hoping to give them a second chance. What a story! If he can be reinvented, so can you! It just takes a plan, effort, and time.

Back to thinking through our reactions with courage; I have been guilty of not doing this successfully at times. Early in my career, I would respond to almost everything that did not agree with my core ethics and values. Remember, before I did the work to become my authentic self, I was the quiet one in the meeting, overanalyzing whether or not to say something. However, when something really rubbed me the wrong way, what first came to my mind sometimes came out of my mouth. In meetings, emails or conversations, I would respond emotionally. Thinking afterwards, "Did I do that?" in my "Steve Urkel" voice. It took one of my respected team members and a peer to pull me aside and share their feedback. I accepted the information and requested they partner with me to help me to improve my responses.

I requested them to pay close attention to my emails and when they saw one that was an example of "what not to send", I asked to have it returned to me with a comment about what I needed to revise. With their help, I was able to see exactly what I needed to change.

When authoring important emails, I began to save them in my Outlook draft folder before hitting the send button. This practice gives me an opportunity to re-read the email prior to sending to find a better, more thoughtful and sometime courageous, way to share information. I take time to evaluate how the information will be received and also to proofread. I am thankful for feedback and see it as a gift that keeps on giving.

In the workplace, there are common negative emotions we might experience that cause us to respond without being thoughtful. We may become unglued when we are frustrated, aggravated, disappointed or nervous. Nonetheless, we must be able to control ourselves. Try my **3T** framework before you go off the deep end.

- **T**ake a deep breath and think about your response before you speak. If you have an opportunity, write a quick note so you can see on paper what you are about to say.
- **T**ransform your mind to look for something positive with what is happening and focus on that. Think about how you can correct the situation as opposed to focusing on the situation itself.
- **T**ip your hat (figuratively) as you leave the room to take a break from the situation. If you are in a meeting, get up, smile and leave. If you can go for a quick walk, to a breakroom or anywhere to take a moment and release. Do not make what could be a permanent decision from a temporary emotion. Be careful when making decisions in emotion, the tradeoff is rarely worth it.

CASE STUDY #15: THINKING THROUGH EMOTIONS IN THE WORKPLACE

One of my mentees really wanted to be promoted but she did not have the sponsorship or advocates needed for it to happen. She had the skills and experience but again, the support was lacking. After finding out this information, I felt the need to be honest and give some very difficult feedback. Because I knew her and wanted her to succeed, I tried to deliver this news in the most caring way; however, after our conversation, she broke down and cried. She could no longer hold in her emotions. I was honored she felt safe enough to express herself but I do not believe a man would break down because he did not have sponsorship.

As the leader, my reaction was also important. I acknowledged her emotions, showed compassion, gave her a tissue, some water, and tried to console her all while allowing her to keep her dignity. It was quite awkward waiting for her to compose herself so I suggested we reconvene later to continue the discussion.

Hindsight is usually perfect sight, but here is what she could have used as another approach to that situation.

1. Tactfully excuse yourself from the meeting
2. Go to the restroom in a stall and pull yourself together

I've had a similar experience as the case study above. A few ways I've handled emotional work meetings are shared in the cart below.

Scenario 1	Politely excused myself from the room, walked down the hallway to the breakroom, made a cup of coffee, used the 3T framework, and rejoined the meeting.
Scenario 2	Politely excused myself from the room, called a confidant to talk for a few minutes where I might discuss the situation or something else. This breaks helps to ground me and move forward.

As team members, we must take responsibility for ourselves and our happiness at work. In the example above, instead of being emotional, the mentee could have developed a plan to find a sponsor. If a situation is not working for you, be empowered to change it.

Another story I will share is about controlling emotions, but it also addresses sexism and being flexible. This true story takes place in Bangalore, India. The transportation company where I worked, afforded me the opportunity to travel around the world. I had been fortunate enough to travel to Germany, Paris, Hong Kong, Singapore and many other places outside and inside the United States. In this case, I was a part of a global leadership cohort helping select non-governmental companies within the Bangalore area. I was the only brown person, as well as the only woman, on my team. Also when wearing the native attire, I could somewhat blend in as a local.

In order to create solutions for our project, we had to visit one of the villages to conduct some research. Upon arrival, I found it was a male dominated world. The non-profit we were helping had a woman as the CEO thus I thought India was modernized from a working woman perspective. One of the men from the company accompanied us to make introductions to the leadership of the company within the village. Again, it was male dominated and all supervisors and workers were men. I did not think it odd because the CEO of the company in the city was a woman. They shook the hands of the men but no one acknowledged me or shook my hand. I thought they just did not hear my greeting. I shared my ideas, they did not make eye contact and dismissed what I was saying; I was inflamed with fury.

I had been in India almost two weeks and this had never happened. I wanted to jump up and shout, "What's wrong with you? It's 2013! Women are in the workplace and running companies now." I had to suppress my emotions, adjust my thoughts and remain calm. It is important to control your emotions, decide your course of action and execute.

I decided not to diminish myself but chose to insert myself into the conversation by using an alternative course of action. My voice was still heard and they knew the ideas were mine because I would whisper them to my male co-worker and, in turn, he would share the information. I later found out that in the villages, they still held longstanding traditions and not as modernized as I had hoped. But the point of the story is I did not become unhinged; I made lemonade out of the lemons I had. We were able to complete our recommendations and our non- governmental agency was able to expand their market. The company had significant growth and was featured in a local business magazine because of our recommendations.

On a side note, if you are ever offered the opportunity to work or travel abroad, seriously consider it. It broadens your horizons and you can experience how people live in other countries. The people in Bangalore were very resourceful and happy. The obstacles I face in the U.S. are minor to some of the things I saw in India, yet, the people were happy just to be alive and filled with joy. Whatever circumstance we may find ourselves in, think of something that makes us happy and grateful and respond in an unemotional, constructive, and respectful way.

Being emotional is not all bad. We are human beings with emotions, however, we must be cognizant of our feelings and think them through with courage and be intentional with our responses.

EXERCISE #16 – AM I EMOTIONAL?

INSTRUCTIONS: How can you tell if you are an emotional person? Work through the exercise below to gain some insight. If most of your answers are yes, you are probably on the emotional side.

	Yes	No
You are very careful not to hurt feelings		
Do you cry easily?		
In a group, when a negative comment is made, do you think they are talking about you?		
Do you laugh nervously?		
You are not afraid to make mistakes		

CASE STUDY #16: REACTIONS WITH COURAGE

Throughout my 25+ years of working in a corporate business environment, I have had the opportunity to coach and mentor both women and men and found some of our reactions are sometimes premature. One of my past team members would react to everything. In one of my staff meetings, someone mentioned they heard the company was going through a layoff. Someone asked, "Will the new people be laid off first?" One of the newer, but not the newest employees in the room, assumed the question was related to her specifically even though no names were mentioned. So she asked the question, "Are you talking about me?" The question in my mind was "Why are you so emotional, in this meeting, at this time?" Again, there were no names called and three other people in the room newer than she. She did not think through the statement or her response. She jumped to a victim mentality and reacted too quickly; she did not let things digest or try find a positive in the situation. I have learned that sometimes things work out without any reaction. It is a great idea to get as many facts as possible around a situation and then react or respond. It is also important to watch the timing of your response. Sometimes you can get stuck in fact finding and never address the situation. There is a happy medium.

January 11, 2009, at 3:00 a.m., I received a call. No one calls at 3:00 a.m. unless it is an emergency. My children and husband were in bed. I had talked to my parents and brothers earlier in the day so I could not imagine what could be happening. If it were a wrong number, I was going to be furious. However, it was my baby brother telling me that our middle brother, Charles Jr. or "Big Charlie", as he was called, had been killed in a drive-by on the freeway in Birmingham, Alabama as he was on his way home from his birthday party. Both of my brothers were at the party but got in their respective cars and went separate ways. We were considered the three musketeers and I was the leader of the crew.

We had never had anything like this to happen before. As a normal middle-class family, this tragic event devastated us. Being the oldest, I had the responsibility of calling my parents to tell them the news. The case was on *The First 48*, which was an actual blessing because it gave us, the family, a bit of assurance that every stone was being turned to solve my brother's murder. The case was solved but going through an investigation, a trial, hearing witnesses, and testimonies was draining as well as life changing. For me, this was an event that sent me to a place I had never experienced.

When I share with you about understanding your emotions, bringing your whole self to work and being who you are, it is something I have had to really work through. At work, I tried to be normal, think through my emotions and model the way for my team but it was hard.

All our experiences make us who we are. Do not just go through the experiences, learn from them, journal about them, and use what you have learned to help others.

Mental health is something not often talked about, especially in the African American community, but it can be a core issue when you are not your whole self with your emotions out of balance. When it was suggested to me that I talk to someone, I brushed it off, saying, "I'll be fine." But I wasn't fine.

God had a way of taking care of me when I couldn't take care of myself. He sent me to an executive coach, Dr. Frank, who was also a licensed psychiatrist. Through our sessions, Dr. Frank helped me to understand many things and introduced me to business concepts and techniques I still use today, for which I am very thankful. He also helped me to identify and understand mild depression and what can be done about it. I did the work and have moved forward successfully. I am sharing with you so when you experience setbacks, disappointments, changes, and tragic events, remember it is not the end of the world. You can move forward if you do the work. If you need assistance, do not brush it off, be proactive and have the courage to seek help. You may continue to function without assistance but it is not likely you will be at your peak or your best self.

Before I did the work, I had fallen into several traps. I have been guilty of speaking too soon and not thinking things through, not understanding the meaning behind a question or a statement. I had to learn through tough experiences, but you do not have to go down the same road to learn the same lessons to be successful in your career. Use the information, strategies, and tips found in this book. Apply what you have learned; you can charter new territory and cross new ground. Then you will be able to share those experiences with others.

There are occasions where you must have the courage to speak truth to power or share bad news with a colleague. Be sure to do so with tact and empathy. When people know you care and are considerate, they receive things differently. It takes courage to deliver bad news. But with a plan, courage, and forethought, the person receiving the news can sometimes make lemonade out of the lemons.

CHAPTER 7

HAVING THE COURAGE TO CONTINUE

In early September 2022, a FedEx delivery driver rang my doorbell and left a package. I opened the box and it was a 25th anniversary gift from the company where I worked. Receiving the package caused me to reflect on my life, trials, and triumphs. I have to admit, it was quite an emotional experience. As I looked back over the 25 years, which was half of my life at the time, I raised my children, traveled the world, made great friends (and some adversaries), and created some revolutionary solutions for customers. Also during those 25 years, I had grown, matured, and learned many lessons, many of the professional ones I have shared in this book.

As I journaled, I realized there were some life lessons worth sharing.

- *Be curious and kind* – Always have an open mind; be open to the gift of feedback and face challenges with questions. In 2016, I was promoted to Director at a Fortune 500 company and was faced with moving to a new state, beginning a new discipline, and assuming a new level of leadership. I had a curious mindset, asked questions and tried to be kind to everyone. As a result, I was able to transition successfully. Stay curious.
- *Never assume* – Assuming will get you in trouble almost every time. Ask questions and validate assumptions with facts.
- *Know and stay true to yourself* – Understand, embrace, and use your uniqueness to benefit yourself and others.
- *Build a network* – Everyone you meet on your journey has a purpose. Working relationships, acquaintanceships and friendships are priceless.

- *Enjoy the journey* – You will miss the beauty of life if you push through without stopping to embrace and enjoy.
- *Give back* – Build the bridge for others to cross and then help them cross it. As you volunteer or give back, learn new or hone current skills. Communicate your success. You can use the examples in Chapter 5 to frame your communication.

It does not matter where you start. Just start. For me it was Bell Sumpter, Alabama. But with a roadmap, tireless effort on your part, and a great support system, you can go anywhere. As I shared at the beginning of the book, I set out with my brother on a journey from Alabama to California. All we had was a roadmap. Back then there were no cell phone or GPS. It was us and the map. A career roadmap is very helpful. You will be more successful with a written, agile guide to help you navigate the corporate highway.

As I reflected, I was interrupted by one of my reverse mentors calling. He had the dilemma of deciding between two excellent job opportunities and sought my advice. As we talked, he created a pros and cons spreadsheet, but was still undecided. I finally asked him, "What are your long-term goals? Where is your career roadmap?" I continued by asking if he accepted either offer, would it be a stop on his career roadmap? He looked at it and only one of the opportunities got him closer to his long-term goals. That was his decision.

"When you understand who you are, what you are passionate about, and set your goals, you have the pieces to build your roadmap to success."

My evolving journey has allowed me to find my passion, which is mentoring and coaching others in business. To bring my passion to life, in 2021 I volunteered and partnered with a family member, with a similar passion, to create the annual "All In One - Women in Business Summit" in Birmingham, Alabama. Our goal was to share business information and empower women to become business owners and leaders.

I have collaborated with other minority women leaders to create an internal company mentorship program to help African American women move from mid-level management to senior leader positions. I love the work I do in helping bring revenue into the corporation but I also love the fact that my company embraces my passion and sees a mutual benefit. Again, it does not matter where you start, just get started on your roadmap guided journey!

On your journey, you will need mentors, your choir of advocates and sponsor-lead singer to help you be successful. Strategically seek out a support system and create as many ally's as you can along the way. As you build your support system, make sure you have the support of your immediate leader. If you don't have the support of your immediate manager, use the techniques in this book to change the situation, if needed.

As you determine your next steps and an interview is a part of the process, I shared extensive information that can help if practiced and implemented. Remember, there is an art to interviewing, so practice is key. Sometimes your entire future depends on that one- or two-hour interviewing session. Study the techniques provided, nail the interview, and prevail in getting the job. By the way, many of the interview tips and techniques can be used for any job interview.

Successfully navigating corporate America is not a walk in the park but it can be done. As I published this book, I am living in my purpose, continuing to work in a corporate setting while mentoring college students, team members and leaders in business. I consult for small businesses in the areas of marketing, information technology and DEI initiatives. I write books and speak at various engagements.

My hope is you will take information from this book you can use and incorporate into what already works for you to guide you to success. Over the course of my career, I have worked with some amazing people, taken and implemented the good traits found in leaders I admire.

I had the courage to continue because I wanted to pave the way for others. I wanted to endure and document experiences so it would not be as hard for others to find success in business. I had the courage to continue for all the first-generation corporate professionals. Hopefully, in these pages, you will see you are not alone and you gain confidence to be successful.

I have evolved, suffered losses, experienced disappointments, achieved successes, and blossomed at different points in my life. And I am still learning and growing. All of those experiences make me, me. All the experiences you had or will have, in your lifetime, will make you, you. My hope for you is that you will:

- Have the **courage** to be the inspiration you are meant to be. Be who you are; own your uniqueness; own your power and know you are ENOUGH!
- Have the **courage** to tactfully and thoughtfully speak up, share the good or bad news and share your bold ideas. Use the 3T framework, if needed, to get yourself and others back on track when hearing uncomfortable information.
- Have the **courage to continue** to keep pursuing your dreams and blaze trails for the next generation. Have the **courage to continue** to pay it forward.

My path is not your path but the corporate business world presents us with a common ground to connect. I trust you found something within this book that feels familiar, something that you are able to connect to. I challenge and encourage you to take it one step further by not just helping others through the gift of experience-sharing or sharing this book, but by also reaching back to open up the door for someone else.

My hope is that you have **THE COURAGE TO JUST CONTINUE!** Good luck!

ENDNOTE

1   https://hbr.org/2019/12/why-dont-women-self-promote-as-much-as-men page 67.

PERSONAL ACKNOWLEDGEMENTS

To my wonderful husband, Carlton, thank you for holding me up when I am falling down and keeping me grounded at all times. You are the wind beneath my wings in God's atmosphere. I love and appreciate you more than words can adequately express.

To my amazing young adult children, Alexandria and Rashad, the two of you have taught me patience and selflessness through my motherhood journey and shown me immeasurable love, patience and understanding. I love you both. Thank you for the blessing of being your mother.

To my God fearing and ever praying parents, Charles and Mary Bevelle, Sr., thank you for bringing me into this world and instilling in me the love of God, the drive to fight for what's right and to do what's right even when no one is watching. I love and cherish you two.

To my brother Michael, you have grown up to be an awesome man and father. Stay true to who you are and continue to give as God has given you. Love you.

To the memory of my brother, Charles E. Bevelle, Jr., as well as my aunts, Charlie Mae Hendrix and Carolyn Hendrix Richardson, my grandfather Cicero Bevelle, Sr., my grandma Katie Mae Bevelle, and my Big Mama, Hattie Ann Hendrix. Although you all have gone home to be with the Lord, you are forever in my heart and part of the force that drives me to be better, each and every day.

To the countless mentors and advocates, who have helped pave the way for me in the world of corporate America, thank you for your guidance and wisdom. Your words, support, and selfless acts of kindness have been key in my success. This book is my way of paying it forward and paving the way for others, as you all have done for me. Special thank you to Angie Jones who helped to guide me through enhancing this book. I could not have done it without your expertise.

~Cheryl~

Printed in the United States
by Baker & Taylor Publisher Services